Acknowledgements

Thanks to my precious family; Sharon my wife; my
children, Alex, Sophia, Sarah and Sarai.
You are all truly a gift to my life. Thank you
for being there for me throughout the years.
It is the love of God through you that has helped me
to stop bleeding and enabled me to help thousands
to stop bleeding also.

Thanks also to the best mother in the world, Etheline
McLean, my 'little' brother Glen,
my sister Janet, my covenant friends
(you know who you are) and my extended family Yahweh
Christian Fellowship International.

Last but not least, my greatest friend,
Jesus Christ,
thank you!

Introduction

If you have found the courage to even open this book, I commend you. This is because many people in life have been trained and indoctrinated to live in unreality, to pretend that everything is fine without ever taking the time to address the genuine issues they face. In a very strange and profound way, pain is one of the universal experiences that humans can identify with. Nations, communities and opposing political parties are often united, even if it is for a brief moment, through pain. Corporate displays of grief have seen people irrespective of ethnicity and religion put aside differences. We can all identify with pain. However, the paradox of pain is that even though it is common, it is unique in every case. This uniqueness means that even though you might be my best friend, father or mother you can only partially empathise with what I am going through and the pain I am feeling. The result of this is that many of us bury our pain, hurts and hide our wounds. We are the 'get over it generation', the 'pull yourself together generation' but there must be a day when we stop 'bleeding'.

The blood in our bodies is one of the most important components of our health. Blood carries oxygen and other vital supplies to all parts of the human body, removes carbon dioxide and helps to defend the body against infection. We all need blood and when we lose blood our body reacts to let us know that an important aspect of its make-up is being discharged. But very few people want to admit they are 'bleeding'. Our life is in our blood and for some of us; our life is slipping away from us. I use the term 'internal bleeding' to describe those life issues that drain our strength, hinder our confidence, destroy our dreams and keep us bound. Internal bleeding in most cases must be treated as an emergency, as continued bleeding can cause death. Internal bleeding is unique in that it is much harder to detect in comparison to external bleeding where people can see the result of a damaged blood vessel. **However, when our external skin is not broken, how do you know if you are bleeding inside?**

I am convinced that we have all 'bled' at some stage in our life and there is no shame in this. In fact whenever we have a physical wound our blood contains tiny particles called platelets which helps our blood to clot, thus preventing too much blood being lost from the body. But what do you do if your blood doesn't clot?

My sincere desire is that through reading this book, you will be able to stop bleeding inside and begin the journey back to wholeness. You may have experienced trauma or be expertly hiding a wound. Many great people hide their true feelings behind what they do. Everybody needs a place where they can rest but if you are bleeding you need to take the time to address the issue. On many occasions, it is the people who are Leaders, Motivators, Ministers, Counsellors, Carers, Teachers and Parents who bleed the most. This is usually because the people that have benefited from their lives expect them to display and demonstrate their gift on a regular basis. You could say that the most vulnerable people are those amongst us who are the greatest 'givers', those whose heart and desire is to help others.

When you visit your local doctor how many times do you ask him or her "are you well"? The truth is we generally expect the physician to heal themselves or at least to know when they require medicine. When I first got married my wife and I signed up with the local doctor. We had a good relationship with her and to this day we are grateful for her support with our first child. However, she developed what appeared to be an insignificant wound and didn't get it treated in time. Her blood became infected and she sadly passed away. Surely an experienced doctor would have known the correct procedures but just because we are great at helping others to stop bleeding doesn't mean we are great at detecting when we are bleeding ourselves! It is only a matter of time before something or someone exposes what is really going on inside. We all have 'triggers' on the inside and we often cannot predict when they will be pulled.

This book will take you on a journey of real life experiences and hope. You will be encouraged to add value to your life by adding more time in your diary for yourself in order to ensure that your body, soul and spirit are well. Your mind is one of the most complex things on the earth simply because it possesses an unlimited ability to think, rationalise, to store and to dream a multitude of things. In its complexity, the mind must be renewed to think correctly. If you operate your life based on wrong thinking you are going to produce the wrong results. Many people in order to survive in life, live each day quoting the words "No pain, no pain, no pain". Regardless of what they are feeling, they set their minds to tell their bodies not to react to any sense of pain. Their thinking and their words have made them numb. Following a recent trip to my dentist, half of my mouth was completely numb due to the work that was carried out. I had to be very careful not to bite and cut my lips because the dentist's injection had made them numb. I was almost oblivious to any pain in my mouth. Shutting pain out has long-term implications and causes people to 'bleed' as they internalise their emotions.

As you will discover through reading this book, internal bleeding can go undetected for a period of time, that is why I am challenging leaders, managers, ministers, entrepreneurs, 'superstars', teenagers, mothers and fathers to read this book as part of their internal examination. It has been proven that in some cases internal bleeding can stop spontaneously but in most cases internal bleeding will not stop without examination and surgery. I am not a medical doctor but I pray that my experiences as a Pastoral carer and Mentor over the years will help you to stop bleeding. You will be encouraged to identify people who can help you through your process of healing and breakthrough. Not everyone around you right now are experienced enough to help you. When someone collapses due to internal bleeding, it is important to be very careful because if you move the person incorrectly, you could cause there to be additional pressure on and compression of, their vital organs, subsequently causing death. **Skilled people must be actioned to help you.**

This book is divided into three sections.

Diagnosis: Identifying and recognising your true condition through signs and symptoms.

Preparing for surgery. Your attitude will effect your prognosis: Looking ahead to how you can recover and what you can do to improve those chances.

Surgery: Applying the tools that will help to improve your overall well being and function.

Read this book initially for YOU, if you are not bleeding then maybe the insight you will receive will enable you to help someone else to stop bleeding.

Love

Rev Noel McLean

Some of the Time

How are you as a person some of the time? I have realised that in counselling people, root issues were often revealed in how they thought and behaved some of the time. I remember counselling a young man who appeared happily married and content most of the time. However, it was revealed that some of the time he would lose all sense of discipline and become embroiled in the most unsavoury situations. Eventually I realised those few mad moments were hiding years of pain and frustration. Generally speaking, we all have moments we wish we would have acted differently but when those moments increase in frequency we should be come very concerned.

The things we struggle with some of the time can have four key elements.

Starting points.

Every issue has a starting point and can often be activated by an act, a word or a thought. We can be the instigator or the recipient of actions, words or thoughts. Many times people are not aware of the series of events that have started in their lives from a particular point.

TURNING POINTS.

Every issue can turn for the better or for the worse. Issues, by nature, have moments when they can be resolved or when they grow to our detriment. Many people I have counselled had no idea of when those turning points were and how close they were to a solution and a major breakthrough. I have often found in relationship counselling, that every couple have a turning point moment, when if seized and maximised, can change their relationship for the better but if ignored, could bring their relationship to a breaking point.

DEFINING POINTS.

Every issue can potentially redefine our lives. This is normally the moment when it becomes clear to you that this issue has marked your life in a way that has changed your perception of your self and people's perception of you. Defining moments can be positive or negative. A mother can look back on the birth of her first child and know it was a defining moment from which she would now be known as a mother. Similarly, a prison inmate can look back on a crime he or she committed and know from that moment they were sentenced, they would have a prison record.

BREAKING POINTS.

When issues have brought us to breaking point, it means that we are at our most vulnerable. Something is breaking inside of us without repair and unless the process is stopped, dreams, visions and hope for things can die within us.

It is often the things we do some of the time and the emotions we display some of the time, that reveal the true condition of our hearts. There are times when we act out of character and rightly say "sorry" but saying sorry, must not mask truth. Is it possible that frequently saying sorry for an uncharacteristic display of emotion is confirmation of a deeper issue? Is it possible you are bleeding inside?

Please read this poem with an open heart and begin to bring your life under the microscope.

Most of the time,
I'm serving others,
providing resources for children, fathers and mothers.
I am gifted to help families
and reconcile members who have become an anomaly.
Some of the time,
I wish someone could do the same for me,
you know, provide kind words and help me face life's enemies.
For I carry the weight of everyone's expectation,
And cannot find the time to address my personal situation.
Most of the time,
I'm a great leader, inspiring others to achieve their goals,
stirring up the potential that resides within their souls.
Clothes washed and committed to doing the school run.
I know what my children need each day,
I will never stop giving to them, come what may!
Some of the time,
When the house is empty and I'm alone,

I sense a pain that is my own.
I'm pretending to be strong when I know I'm not,
But who can help me move from this emotional spot?
Some of the time, In a secret place,
I cry out for someone to help me win my own race.
I can hear for others and see for some
but for myself, it seems like my breakthrough will never come.
Most of the time, I am the perfect mum,
Cooking the dinners and organising the school run,
Some of the time, the pressure is too much,
But who do I go to, for that special touch?

Most of the time,
I'm the person of faith,
Walking in love and God's perfect grace.
I can believe for the impossible,
And through faith appear invincible.
Some of the time,
I'm afraid to see,
The real challenges that are going on inside of me.
I love God, so I will never quit,
But ministering to others and not myself makes me seem like a hypocrite.
Most of the time,
I am the peacemaker,
Keeping my family and friends together.
I seem to be the bridge for others,
To find their way through troubled waters.
Some of the time,
I am really hurting,
From the words of others, I have been helping.
I need a few moments just for myself
To make sure my needs don't stay on the shelf.

Most of the time,
Money is no problem; I own my own company and have so many life options.
I socialise with the rich and attract attention,
And pride myself on my great reputation.
Some of the time,
I feel like I'm dying.
Every time I smile in front of a camera, I feel like I'm lying.
I'm tired of playing this game because I know I'm cheating,
Not even my closest friends would sense that inside I'm bleeding.

Who Am I?

Where you told who you are or did you discover who you are? How do you decide who is right? As human beings we look at the world from a subjective point of view. We analyse and interpret events through the filter of our minds and experiences. When we take time to discover more about whom we are and the type of person people see in us, it will invariably help us to understand why certain events affect us and other events do not. Why certain things people say to us affect us and other things people say do not. Why we find it easy to forget certain incidents in our lives and then struggle with others.

Most of us tend to fall into what is termed as 'personality types'. The following is only a guideline and not exhaustive but designed to help you know yourself better.

Type A personality

These people tend to be very competitive in nature and can therefore come across as being overpowering. They tend to be hurried in their approach to life and will push themselves for fast and sometimes immediate results. They are people who tend to believe that the end justifies the means.

Type B personality

These people tend to be very optimistic regarding the world. They are friendly and believe that most people have the capacity to do good. They are generally patient and try to maximise the opportunities they have now rather than thinking too much about the future. These are people that are generally open and willing to discuss and work through issues if they are of a critical nature. In psychology they are termed as being more 'right brain' dominated, which means they are intuitive and tend to use humour to express their anger

Type C personality

These people tend to be introverts and will carefully and methodically consider decisions before they are made. They are careful planners and think a lot about the future and how best to prepare for it. They tend to process difficult issues on their own and when upset find it easier to go silent and shut down emotionally. They are regarded as being 'left brain' orientated which means they tend not to be very open about their emotions and even though they can be very gifted their approach to relationships do not always make them great leaders.

Personality, can be broadly defined as being our innate characteristics, who we are genetically. Our personality is who we distinctively are as a person. Character, can be broadly described as being the traits, attitudes and behaviour we develop through life that become associated with our personality. If these definitions are true, it is important to know that it is highly unlikely that anyone will change your personality and therefore unlikely you will be able to change anyone else's. It is possible to be around someone who has a personality that you find challenging but their characteristics are loving and caring. This means our personality can have a bearing on the success or failure of relationships, how people initially perceive us, how we feel around people and how people feel around us.

Hopefully you will begin to understand yourself a little better and depending on your personality type, why you might be bleeding. My desire is for you to not only identify where and why you are bleeding but to understand the systems you need to put in place to protect your heart.

How might you react to someone telling you that you have a serious inner issue? Look at the following assumptions for various personality types to five key questions

Question	TYPE A	TYPE B	TYPE C
Do you have a problem with relationships?	Hostile	Friendly	Cautious
Do you have a personal problem?	Critical of it	Open to it	Sensitive to it
Can you change your diary?	Rigid	Flexible	Inflexible
What is your attitude towards change?	Negative	Inevitable	Discomfort
How do your react emotionally when something makes you really happy?	Guarded	Open	Hidden

Your thoughts affect yours ways. It is almost impossible for someone's ways to change without them experiencing a change in their thought life. A man becomes the product of his thoughts. Often it is our 'belief' system that prevents us from acknowledging areas of our lives that need attention. What type of internal system is within you? I would suggest to you that every one of us has a system that is made up of plugs, filters and holes.

Filters: These are the past experiences we have had in our lives that filters everything around us. When someone speaks to us, when someone carries out a course of action it is automatically filtered and produces explanations and reasons. As a qualified engineer, I was used to using various types of filters. Oil filters, water filters and many more. Filters, will remove things in its path that are deemed harmful or unwanted by the user or system. However, if the wrong filter is fitted it can **remove things that are crucial to the smooth running of the system**. Our personal filters can often hear a genuine word of encouragement, filter those words and believe the words are patronising.

Plugs: These are thoughts, mindsets and actions that we use to bring temporary relief from problems and the challenges of life. Plugs can hold back a problem for a season. Plugs are useful but they are only intended as a temporary fix and over a period of time will give way to the things they are holding back. There are some people that spend most of their lives changing their plugs rather than finding a resolution to a problem.

Holes: These are the things that we need for everyday life. Holes allow us to release tension and get rid of unwanted things in our lives. Holes can also be areas of our lives that cause us to lose valuable strength and resources. It is important **not to plug a hole that is intended to bring release**. Many people have been encouraged not to share their problem or told to put a 'cap' on it. This results in them internalising instead of releasing. One of the most damaging things that you can do to someone you are in relationship with, **is to prevent them from talking,** sharing their concerns.

Why is it important to know what personality type you are and what type of system you have?

The main reason is that as you are taken on a journey through this book, you will begin to understand why certain areas of your personality, life style and mindsets are challenged. Challenge is often the prerequisite for change and change is often sustained by new habits. I have found through years of Pastoral care, that some people resist change unknowingly because they are not aware of who they really are.

I was once asked to counsel a successful business man who was experiencing a lot of inner turmoil. During the session, nearly everything I suggested in order to challenge some of his clear areas of bleeding was met with "but I am so successful". At the end of our first session he asked me "are you going to pray that everything goes away now before I leave"? I soon realised this man had applied his personality and his system into our meeting and that unless he was willing to be challenged, I wouldn't be able to help him. Unfortunately he never came to see me again!

Knowing who you are can be a great advantage to your healing. Every day we receive thousands of words that depending on who we are, invariably carry different semantics. We also have a plethora of challenges that will cause us to respond in different ways. This book provides you with a great opportunity to address your areas of bleeding and move forward in healing. If you stood in an identity parade would you know yourself? Identity parades are used to help victims identify perpetrators. However, the unique feature of the identity parade is that suspects are often of a similar ethnicity, height and build. The victim has to then identify the perpetrator based on what mental images they retain. It is so important that you don't allow the challenges of life to form mental images in your mind that are not a true reflection of yourself.

Once you know who you are, you may find that for the first time in your life you are able to make choices with your personal welfare and well-being in mind. The great thing about making choices is that it indicates that authority is back in your own hands. Many people who have been victims suffer due to an abuse of power and authority in someone-else's hand. If you cannot trust the authority of someone you are in relationship with, then you have to question the value of the relationship. I define choice as the power to reveal a preferred path.

Who am I test

1. **I am who I am by design.** There are genetic traits that influence who you are. The way you were created and what characteristics you were born with. You can often see yourself in your mother, father or relatives.

2. **I am who I am by circumstance.** Circumstances are those determining factors around us that are not necessarily within our control. Circumstances can impact our core being. Many people try to change their circumstances in order to see changes in themselves.

3. **I am who I am by choice.** Choice is the power to determine various factors in our lives. A deliberate decision to be someone. You are able to take full responsibility for who

you are now. Choice is a gift that only benefits us when it is used with wisdom.

4. **I am who I am by influence.** Influence is the power to affect a person; to change a thing and determine an outcome. Our personal peer group can play a very significant role in our lives and can inspire positive or negative behaviour in us. The outcomes of major challenges in our lives are often related to those people that influenced our thought process throughout.

5. **I am who I am through dictatorship.** This means that you are who you are, by virtue of someone who has absolute authority over your life with no permitted opposition. This can be oppressive but many times we inadvertently 'appoint' people into a position we regret.

Who you have become, can often be the reason why you are bleeding.

Key

1 Challenge the mental images you have of yourself.
2. Don't be afraid to change your filters.
3. Know your personality and begin to see your personality as a plus not a minus.

1 Cor 13:12 " For now I see in a mirror, dimly, but then face to face".

Help I'm Bleeding!

From a medical perspective internal bleeding is defined as being bleeding that takes place inside the body. It can be caused by many things ranging from high blood pressure to cancer. Serious car accidents that rupture lungs and blood vessels can also cause internal bleeding. Generally speaking, if internal bleeding is not stopped it can eventually cause death. This is because internal bleeding can make vital organs dysfunctional. Internal bleeding can go undetected for some time and even those trained as medical practitioners, would find it hard to diagnose without medical instruments and an internal examination.

In the medical world, the following are keys signs of internal bleeding but this list is not exhaustive.

Fast and weak pulse rate.
Pale skin.
Confusion and disorientation.
Bleeding from mouth.
Blood in urine.
Cold and clammy skin.
Marks or fresh bruises on abdomen or skin.

Conversely, I would suggest that there are some key signs from a Pastoral perspective that would suggest internal bleeding but as mentioned, the list is not exhaustive.

Continued frustration with life. "I am just fed-up". Continual frustration can indicate that you are stuck in an emotional place that is draining your strength.

Continued double-mindedness. "Maybe I should, or perhaps I shouldn't". Uncertainty within us is often tied to the fluctuations of our damaged emotions.

Inability to trust. "I just cannot commit, it is too good to be true". The inability to trust often stems from old emotional wounds.

Imbalanced life style. "I haven't got time to rest". Working to the point of exhaustion helps to block out reality but living in unreality can cause long-term physical and emotional damage.

Continual lack of confidence. "Just not sure if I can do it". When you lack confidence, you fail to see yourself achieving anything of significance. Previous disappointments have filled your heart with doubt.

Inner judgments. "They are all the same". You have already prejudged a person or a situation before you even know the facts because of how you are feeling. It is hard for you not to pre-judge a situation when the majority of things in your history confirm your judgement is justified.

Unhealthy attachments. "I just need……..". Many times we cling to people and things, not because we need them but because needing something or someone, temporarily displaces inner pain.

We all face challenges every day in our careers, home life and vocations and not all issues in our lives can be termed as being serious. However, threats are more that just challenges because they put our well-being at risk. Everyone at some stage in their life needs to scrutinise and test their hearts to see if they are well and to know what actions need to be taken in order to stop what might initially be a minor issue becoming a major issue.

I remember several years ago, whilst on a ministry trip, meeting a gang leader. I was shocked how young he was. Nevertheless, he had the power to sanction murders. Upon further investigation I realised that for many years in the local area there had been a cycle of gang leaders who had been killed and many of them didn't live beyond twenty one years of age. I will never condone violence but the question is, "was this young gang leader just another man in a long line of people who were bleeding"?

I have been privileged to have ministered in many parts of the world but one conversation with a young war torn girl will never leave me. Whilst evangelising in an area where there were regular shootings and murders, I came across a pretty young girl of about 12 years of age. Her clothes were torn and she was dirty. This young girl had grown up seeing people murdered nearly everyday of her life. When I asked her what I could do to help, she said "the thing I want the most is for the killing to stop". At the age of twelve, this young girl was 'bleeding' and didn't know how to stop. She had been unable to go to school or even play freely on the streets because of the violence.

I know that the devil hates families and marriages but I believe that some relationships have failed because people didn't realise they married someone who was bleeding, the Pastor didn't realise he appointed someone who was bleeding, the manager didn't realise he employed someone who was bleeding, you didn't realise you became close friends with someone who was bleeding and wondered why they became so possessive in their friendship with you and the list goes on. Remember, the first stages of internal bleeding can go unnoticed unless blood comes out through a bodily orifice therefore the person you have introduced into your life may not display any signs of bleeding until an event reveals their condition.

Whenever I read the Bible, I am amazed to discover how much Jesus cared about people who were bleeding. The story of a suffering Woman in Mark 5: 22-43 gives us some important insights about 'bleeding'. Jesus is **first asked** to come and attend to a synagogue rulers' daughter who is at the point of death .However, on His way there, a woman who was haemorrhaging, reaches out to him, touches the hem of his garment and is healed. The truth is that both women were at the point of 'death'. The moment the woman realised that she had stopped bleeding was a turning point in her life. The Bible does not tell us whether it was the woman's fault or not why she had this disease (Matthew 9:20) but the Bible does tell us that she tried everything she knew to stop bleeding. Amazingly despite previous disappointments with physicians she believed if she reached out for help, her bleeding would stop. Regardless of who you are or what you do, it is time you demonstrated the faith to 'touch someone' who can help you? **It is rare that people who are bleeding have the ability to replace the blood they have lost without help.** Not every pain or issue in your life needs immediate attention but when it gets to the stage where the issues are draining you of confidence, enthusiasm and joy then you are bleeding and need immediate help.

When you are bleeding you need to be aware of your motives all the time. "Why am I desperate to get married"?

"Why do I need that promotion"? "Why do I want to go into full-time ministry"? "Why do I need to take drugs"? Are you hoping these things will stop you from bleeding? Never marry someone hoping they will stop you from bleeding. Be careful when your soul reason for making friends with someone is in the hope they can stop you from bleeding as your friends, husband or wife will become a doctor not a soul mate. Many relationships fail because someone within the relationship could not continue to prescribe a cure for someone's bleeding.

It is amazing the way the medical profession classifies different levels of bleeding. Remember I am not a doctor so the following is layman's terms!

Class I Haemorrhage involves up to 15% loss of blood volume. There is typically no change in vital signs and fluid resuscitation is not usually necessary.

Class II Haemorrhage involves 15-30% loss of total blood volume. A patient can often have a rapid heart beat. The body attempts to compensate for this loss however, the skin will often start to look pale and changes in a persons behaviour becomes evident. Volume resuscitation is all that is typically required.

Class III Haemorrhage involves loss of 30-40% of circulating blood volume. The patient's blood pressure drops, the heart rate increases and the mental status worsen. Fluid resuscitation is definitely necessary.

Class IV Haemorrhage involves loss of blood greater than 40% of the circulating blood volume. The limit of the body's compensation is reached and aggressive resuscitation (replacing of lost blood) is required to prevent death.

What class are you in? The reality is that even if you are a Class 1, if you continue to bleed you will soon go into another class. Don't wait until your life reaches a Class 4 and you find you don't have the strength to maintain healthy relationships with your family and friends. To realise and acknowledge that you are bleeding requires great courage but honesty is the universal quality of all true winners and champions!

Everyone needs to cry out for help at some stage in their lives and to reach out for assistance. Your greatest display of courage is often displayed in your humility. The easiest way to receive help is to ask. Don't wait for people to assume what you need or for people to help you by chance. There are times however, when people who love you simply take the initiative to help you. I remember many years ago arriving at a hotel in East Africa on one of my first mission trips. As soon as I arrived at the hotel, the porters took my suitcase even though I was quite happy to bring them upstairs to my room myself. I was never given the choice as to whether I wanted to carry my suitcases or not, I had to submit to the protocol of the Hotel. It is important that you bring yourself into the right protocol where change is inevitable and service is guaranteed. You must have people who you can cry out to and be sure that they can either help you to stop bleeding or point you to someone who can.

There are five presuppositions that are often adopted by people prior to any help received. Which one best describes you?

1. **Cynical**. Are you someone that immediately adopts a negative approach to receiving help? Some people who are cynical have been disappointed many times in the past and therefore adopt a cynical approach to support and change. It's like the alcoholic who sincerely promises

to stop drinking; they are more likely to receive a cynical response from those that have suffered the most from their behaviour. I have found that some cynics deep down, would really like to believe.
2. **Sceptical**. Are you someone that initially doubts but once your questions are answered will move towards a positive mindset? In some cases it is important to be sceptical about support that is offered but you need to be careful that your list of questions doesn't cause you to miss out on the help that is on offer.
3. **Rational.** Are you someone that will not respond to help unless everything makes sense to you? Many times when people identify an area of weakness in your life it may seem illogical to you or hard for you to understand but is there room in your thinking for truth that challenges you?
4. **Pragmatic**. Are you someone that will only approach issues in your life with facts not feelings?
Are you someone that can only work within set systems and ways of doing things? It can sometimes be difficult for pragmatic people to step outside of the norm and embrace change.
5. **Idealist.** Are you someone that lives for the ideal that is formed in your thoughts and find it difficult to accept things outside your ideal? There is nothing wrong in living with an ideal in mind. However, very few people on the face of the earth live out an ideal. Our thoughts need to be renewed on a regular basis so that we can embrace the diversities of life and the people assigned to help us.

One of the most frightening experiences for me happened when one of my daughters at fourteen months, somersaulted off my kitchen table onto our hard kitchen floor. I heard the scream from my wife and ran into the kitchen. Blood was in several places. Initially it was hard to know where my daughter was bleeding from. Was it her head, face or mouth? Upon further investigation we found out it was her lip. If I had followed the blood stains I would had been misled because there was more blood on my daughters cotton T-shirt than her lip. Be aware that the area of your life that might manifest anger and frustration is not necessarily the source of your pain. Many people bleed from their place of pain not from the source of their pain. I remember working with a young man who had a distinct sexual problem. He was married and had shared with me his infidelity. He felt that this area of weakness was destroying him as a person. However, we traced the source of his bleeding to a deep routed rejection he had received within his marriage.

Key

It is almost impossible to change beyond your will. Being consistent is dangerous if you are consistently demonstrating behaviour that denies you help.

Proverbs 4:26 "Consider the path of thy feet and let all thy ways be established".

I Refuse To Cry!

Even if you are not a Christian who reads the Bible on a regular basis, many non-Christians are aware of the shortest verse in the Bible, John 11:35, "Jesus wept". But why did such a great man cry? I am convinced that the most ingenious of beings on earth is Man. We are an amazing work of art; therefore it is important to allow our bodies to function in the way it was designed. When you purchase an electrical item, contained within the owners' manual are directives encouraging the user not to use the item outside its design function so that it does not breakdown. Have you ever considered that when you say "I refuse to cry" that you might just be acting outside of your design?

Jesus cried probably because of the grief he saw Mary and Martha experience after the death of their brother, Lazarus. Whatever the reason was, Jesus experienced a build-up of chemicals and hormones as a result of something that moved him emotionally. Crying releases the excess chemicals that our body does not need during our times of great emotion than can be as a result of grief or pain.

Crying can sometimes be the first step to wholeness when we understand that crying is not a sign of weakness but a sign of our humanness. It is important that you release your pain and not carry the pains of previous events within or they will mount up and destabilise you emotionally. In counselling people I have found that there are five main reasons why people refuse to cry. Do any of them reveal you?

- I refuse to cry in front of the person who hurt me so that they don't have the benefit of knowing they hurt me.
- I made a vow never to allow myself to cry over the same problem again.
- I refuse to cry anymore as I am tired of being weak.
- I ignore and resist the feeling to cry.
- Crying is a waste of time as it is not going to change anything.

Challenge to number 1. Crying is ultimately not for the benefit of the person who has hurt you but for your emotional benefit.

Challenge to number 2. If the problem has re-occurred, refusing to cry will not create the solution.

Challenge to number 3. Crying from a health perspective can actually help you to eventually be strong as you have released stress and tension from your body.

Challenge to number 4. Emotions don't need to be ignored but rather managed.

Challenge to number 5. Time spent crying is not always understood but is never wasted.

I would like to suggest to you that crying is an indication that you are processing pain or displeasure.

Thought

When you consider and contemplate on what someone has done or what you have done, the thoughts then stir an emotion in you.

Response

You cry because you are responding to the actions or events that you have just processed internally.

Genuine tears may not always be understood but they should never be ignored. I am a very proud father of four children and from time to time my little 'angels' surely try my patience! However, I can remember feeling very convicted in my heart when I told two of my children on two separate occasions to "stop crying". I personally did not want any more noise in my tired ears! However, my words had a profound effect on my children over a period of time that has caused me to duly change my approach to my children.

I noticed that on one occasion after being told to "stop crying" my son said to me "but daddy, am I not allowed to be sad?" This touched my heart. Unknowingly, I had caused my son to believe that it was always wrong to express his emotions. In my thoughts, I felt that if he was crying after being corrected about something, it was a sign of rebellion but it was just a sign of a young boy being disappointed. I then noticed that instead of crying in front of me, he would go to his room and cry silently. I would sometime listen outside his door to his tears with a convicted heart! I had to change my approach! There are too many silent criers in the world, people who bleed behind closed doors. Are you one of them?

With my eldest daughter, due to my response to her crying, I noticed that she began to hold back tears in my presence. It was only when I would look closely at her eyes I would notice that there were small indications of tears. I then realised that I would always need to ask her "are you alright?", previously I would always know when my daughter was upset about things! These were important lessons for me. **I had selfishly decided what was and what wasn't worth crying for. The emotions that should flow naturally should not be hindered.** I have known of some mothers who became worried when their new born baby did not cry but may be we should become worried when we or the people we love never cry.

Over the years I have done quite a lot of travelling and the one incident that I find hard to walk past, is a person crying. In the midst of a busy world, your cry is still distinctive and those that truly love you will be willing to help. A thousand tears can make a pool and a million a river.

Key

The next time you sense the need to cry, find a safe environment to do so in order that your process of healing will not be disrupted.

Psalm 30:5. *"weeping may endure for a night but joy comes in the morning"*.

FAKE IT UNTIL YOU MAKE IT!

Most people live in two worlds; the private and the public. Within the public world we try our best to live up to our ideals; the perfect husband or wife, the successful business man or woman, the strong Leader, the list goes on. Every role in life comes with an ideal state of being and these ideals are normally set by our peer groups, job descriptions, self targets, or even our interpretation of the role. People often find ourselves fighting against their ideal and their current state, simply because they appear to be so contrasting. Ideals are often things we work towards as human beings but our current reality challenges us to let go of our ideal. One way in which I have seen people try to reconcile their current reality with their ideal, is to pretend, to fake it until they believe they make it. The word fake describes something that is a distortion or misrepresentation of the genuine.

Being transparent is a choice but it must be two dimensional. People you trust must be able to see through you and into you. In the Bible, Jesus chose to reveal more about his humanity and divinity to Peter, James and John even though he had many other disciples around him. Those three men saw Him in His times of strength and weakness. Your public world has to be a world that you can 'breathe in', make mistakes in and be your self. Have you noticed that as you are climbing a hill or mountain, you need to adjust your breathing because of the change of altitude? The more prominent your life, the greater the adjustments need to be so you can breathe. The hype of this world has influenced our society to the degree that people of greatness lose a sense of reality by maintaining a public image at the expense of genuine happiness. People employ publicists, promoters and media consultants in order to maintain the right reputation. Perception is important but it should never be pursued at the expense of truth.

You must be real, even if it costs you your reputation. Many people unfortunately value the opinions of men above their own needs. Even if you are not a Christian you can learn much from the life of Jesus in the Bible and how He knew people of his day valued their reputations. He employed an incredible strategy which was to make himself of no reputation .How do you not become preoccupied in making a reputation? In the Bible, there are several Greek translations for the word *reputation*, it will be helpful for us to take a brief look at some of them.

> Entimos: Meaning that which is dear, honourable and precious.
> Dokeo: To be noticed or accounted.
> Timios. Valuable, to be held in honour.

We all desire to be **respectively** thought of and **honoured** in some way or form. However, there is another Greek translation of the word *reputation* which is much more relevant to us. It is the Greek word *Kenoo* and it means to 'make empty'. The first step to addressing the real you is to EMPTY YOURSELF of who you are not. It is really hard work trying to pretend you are full and when you are empty. In my household, we drink a lot of water. I often get frustrated that once the water bottles are used no one seems to fill them back up. Therefore I thought I would do a little home experiment. If I left the water bottle full, everyone in the house approached the bottle with the view of taking water from the bottle. However, if I left the water bottle empty on the side of the breakfast table, everyone approached the bottle to fill it with water. The strange thing is that the water bottle was never refilled by my family when it was half full and this meant that at meal time we ran out of nice cold water! However, if it was clear that the water bottle was empty it was usually filled! When it is clear that you are empty, people who genuinely care about you will seek to fill you, not take from you.

Could it be your attempts to look full when you are empty that are attracting the wrong people?

If an Apple tree looked like a Thorn bush it would never attract anyone to its fruit. Many times we don't attract the right people and support because we are not being who we really are. I once did some research into what attracts skunks! I realised that one of the main reasons for attracting skunks is the rubbish that many households leave unprotected. Unfortunately, if we allow people who do not mean well to get close enough to us, they will be attracted to the **unwanted areas of our lives** that are exposed. Therefore don't waste your precious life building something that one headline can tarnish.

Can you do the 'you' test?

Do you freely express your own thoughts or the thoughts of others?
Do you have an image of yourself or are you living in the image someone created for you?
Do you have people around you who could handle three things about yourself that reveal your weaknesses?

Take the time to ask yourself if you are 'faking it' as a wife, husband, mother, teenager, manager or leader. You can only play the part until someone sees you when you're not acting? I love to watch films and when I am not studying, teaching or preaching, I am watching a movie! I also love going to the theatre and I am enthralled by great acting. The discipline of learning and submersing yourself into a character, learning your lines is just amazing to me. The visible nature and personality of the characters I see in these films can very rarely give me any insight into who they really are away from the camera. Many people have learnt their lines so well that even when asked "how are you", they have a standard fake reply!

Away from the camera, away from your job, away from the husband, the wife and work colleagues are you bleeding, how are you"? Yes "How are you"? Often people who are bleeding never answer the question truthfully. Anyone who cannot handle your truth cannot handle the real you. I once bought a phone answering machine. I was amazed to find that there were two types of messages I could record for those calls I missed. An internal message and an external message. The facility is great for people who want to say one message to people outside their company and another message to people within the company but the problem comes when you speak mixed messages to yourself!

ARE YOU NOW USED TO THE WRONG YOU?

It is possible that you can behave in such a wrong way for a period of time that you are now more accustomed to who you are not rather than who you really are. In the unlikely event that you did not have a mirror for 40 days, the only perception of what you look like would in your thoughts. What if your thoughts were not aligned with truth? I remember watching a great children's film where a female woolly mammoth grew up thinking she was a possum! I guess I have madder my point.

Please consider the following. You don't have to be a superstar to have these people in your life. I am not suggesting these roles are evil or unnecessary but it is possible to have people around you who only serve to create something you are not.

PUBLICIST

The general role of a publicist is to be a bridge between their client and the media. They seek to release information to the press and the public arena over a number of years in order to create the desired image for their client. They can even write articles and release information about their client in the hope that it will help their client to be successful.

PROMOTER

The general role of a promoter is to market the events their client is involved in order for the event to be a success. This work may involve hyping up the event amongst the public through the media in order to generate greater interest and excitement.

There are times, when you need to make some people redundant because what they are saying about you is no longer true! Only the genuine will survive the test of time. I have noticed over the years that some celebrities have been willing to pay off an aggrieved individual who threatened to go public with the details of the celebrities' inappropriate behaviour towards them. The celebrity is often encouraged to pay off an individual in order to preserve something or someone they are not. Friends are great to have but the ones who don't tell you the truth can be as lethal as your enemies.

Travelling as I do on a regular basis, I always try and bring back something nice for the family. My son being an avid football fan would always ask me for a football t-shirt of his favourite team. In some of the poor countries I visited, I would buy replica football shirts at a town market. My son loved them and would wear the t-shirts with pride. However, as my son got older he one day said "Dad when you return from your mission, can you try and buy be an original football shirt for my team"? He had reached and age where he could tell what was fake and what was original. I realised that to buy an original t-shirt **would cost me more**. It will always cost you more to be who you are. It will always cost you more to address a problem rather than ignore the problem. It will always cost you more to speak-out rather than remain silent. Anything that is fake is an enemy of the original.

You can play a part as an actor so well that you are not even aware when you are supposed to be 'out of character'. Take a few moments the next time you are walking down a high street filled with shoppers and ask yourself "how many of these people are actually fake"? I was told once of a business promoter who was renting a very poor property to live in but had ploughed all his savings into buying a new Mercedes Benz in order to create the right image. He eventually had to close down his promotion company and ended–up with debts. Lasting success comes from you being you!

As a Person who has various responsibilities in the community, at home and abroad, I am constantly checking myself to ensure that I am not living a lie. Websites these days can transform the image of a company, business and attract new customers. I can recall listening to an outstanding commercial on the radio regarding property consultants. I decided to ring the contact number only to find the phone was answered by someone who was shouting because of a washing machine in the background and who couldn't speak good English. To make things worse, after agreeing an appointment with a consultant, a couple of days before the appointment they decided to talk to me over the phone because they realised it was a bit too far to travel across the city to meet me! Society encourages us to invest our time and money in establishing our image but sometimes we find ourselves in a situation where we cannot afford for people to know the truth! We can all live the dream provided we know what is real and when we are dreaming!

Catch me if you can!

Can anyone really catch the real you? In 2002 Steven Spielberg released a film based on the true story of Frank Abagnale Jr. Frank, before he was nineteen years of age, successfully received and cashed millions of dollars in cheques by pretending to be a pilot, doctor, history teacher and legal prosecutor. Eventually he was arrested and jailed for fraud. It is possible to be many people apart from the person we really are. When was the last time some one caught up with the real you?

In carrying out many short-term mission trips, I have realised that mission is one of the best ways to know what people are really like. There appeared to be two principle things that revealed the true character of a person when on mission. One, was the sense of being stretched outside their 'comfort zone' and two, the sense of being challenged to accommodate the personalities of others on the mission trip. As a teenager, I actually hated the taste of alcohol. However, I was conscious of trying to accommodate the character and habits of my peers. I remember deciding to have a few beers during a party. This was something that was not consistent with my character but I was encouraged to step outside my comfort zone. When I woke up the next morning with a terrible headache, I realised that the person I had tried to be the night before was not the real me. I am not suggesting that my friends controlled me but **sometimes accommodation can lead to impersonation**. Everyone has to make a decision to either be the person in the mirror or the person behind the mask.

Bonus features

One of the selling points of DVD's are the bonus features. I can remember watching one such DVD and decided to watch the bonus features after the film. One of the features showed all the mistakes the actors and actresses made whilst filming that were edited out of the final film. Some of the scenes were hilarious but it made me see the humanity of people who are undoubtedly talented but human. Being the real you can be a bonus, benefit to you and those that genuinely love you.

People who work in banks are trained primarily to know and identify when genuine currency is in their hands in order to identify the false. Your mind now needs to be renewed and transformed in order for you to know who you genuinely are.

Take this first step and address the real you. It's the real 'you' that needs to stop bleeding. Be willing to speak the truth. Be willing to ignore the image people have set for you, and find your ORIGINAL.

You can succeed in life without having to fake your every step. God has placed in us a great destiny and no one can fill your specific footsteps neither should you try to fill others.

KEY

1. Never let anyone who has discussed something with you, leave your presence without them not knowing your view and perspective.
2. Never say yes to someone when you desire to say no, for the sake of impressing.
3. Build relationships with people who love your strengths and can have grace for your weaknesses.
   One of the GREATEST things you can say that will be a catalyst for change is "I cannot live a lie anymore". Every lie will generally run its course until someone stumbles across the truth!

Proverbs 27:5 *"Better is open rebuke and hidden love"*

The Talent Trap

As a musician and a lover of great music, I have often studied the lives of great musicians and singers. I have been overwhelmed by the God given talent many of these individuals had and their unique ability to express their ideas, views and passions. Sadly some of these amazing people fell into what I called the 'talent trap'.

Traps have been used for many years in order to restrain, capture and even kill animals and people. In order to help you understand how the talent trap and other emotional traps work, let us consider three common types of traps used in catching animals.

Killing traps. These are generally traps that are designed to bring a quick and clinical death to the animal caught in the trap. However, if the animal enters the trap the wrong way, it is possible for the animal to remain in a very disturbing state until dead.
Restraining traps. These are generally intended to capture an animal and hold that animal alive in the trap until the trapper has time to arrive and kill the animal.

Snares. These types of traps are considered the most lethal as the trapped animal is held in between two closing plates around the neck or limb. The more the animal struggles to be free from the trap, it is the more the restraint around the animal tightens, reducing breathing or causing excruciating pain. Death in this manner can be long and painful and is considered by many as inhumane!

The talent trap can cause quick or long-term death and often when people have tried to escape, the grip on their lives only tightens. They continue to bleed internally not knowing how to break free as the trap becomes the only way they know how to live.

One of my favourite artists in terms of unique vocal style is Billie Holiday. Even today she is regarded as being one of the outstanding jazz singers of all time. Sadly behind her great talent was a struggle with heroin and alcohol that led to her untimely death. How could someone with so much talent die in such sad circumstances? Did anyone really know what was going in inside Eleanora Gough (this was her real name as Billie Holiday became her professional name)? Was she bleeding inside?

Billie Holliday grew up without a father and had a mother who in some ways caused Billie to feel unloved and insecure. As a consequence Billie had many unhappy relationships and her last album in 1958 was a shadow of the person whose voice had once captivated listeners. A year later Billie collapsed and while on her death bed was sadly placed under arrest for heroin possession.

Another amazing talent was Dorothy Jean Dandridge who coincidently, was earmarked to play Billie Holliday in a film biography but unfortunately the film did not materialise in her life time. Dorothy was not only a talented actress but a fantastic singer and despite the obstacles of racism within society and the acting industry, was a ground- breaker. Dorothy was the first black woman to appear on the cover of Life Magazine and also the first black actress to be nominated for an Oscar as best actress in a leading role. Her talent was clear for all to see but behind the scenes this beautiful woman was bleeding inside. Two marriages that ended in divorce, bad financial management and an ongoing drink problem meant that this amazing woman was hurting inside. It is also thought that she battled depression and at her death only had $2.14 in her bank account.

Karen Carpenter for me had one of the most moving voices I have heard. Her musical partnership with her brother Richard, made a mark in the hearts of people and the music industry during the late sixties, seventies and early eighties. However, despite her ability to reach the hearts of millions with her songs, there was an inner struggle taking place. This talented lady battled with her self image and believing that her weight was not acceptable, battled with anorexia. Anorexia distorts people's self image and causes them to become obsessed with controlling their weight. Success brought a very demanding schedule of rehearsals, travel and performances that may have pushed Karen into trying to keep her weight constant. Externally Karen looked healthy but inwardly something was taking place that would eventually lead to her decline. One of the key things that Karen did, with the help of her brother was to take TIME out. When Karen initially became ill, tours and recording sessions were postponed in order to give Karen time to receive treatment. How many people who sat in the audiences thrilled by her music, knew what was going on inside Karen? Karen eventually lost her fight with anorexia but will you lose your fight? I recently heard a post boxing fight interview with a trainer and he said these profound words, "my fighter lost this fight for all the wrong reasons". It is possible for us to lose the fight for our lives for all the wrong reasons when we believe a lie.

Our talents must not hide truth and our talent must not create a lie. Our talents must not take us where our soul cannot keep us. Billie Holiday and Dorothy Dandridge possessed a talent that many today would crave for but how much more would Billie and Dorothy had preferred to have had peace within their soul? How much pain were they carrying throughout their lives?

Are you trapped by your talent? Do you love your talent more than yourself? The world loves to find talent, expose talent and get pleasure from talent but you're never indispensable to the world. The world will feel sorry for you and then abruptly seek to fill your space. There will be other singers, dancers, millionaires, managers and leaders after you have died but there will never be another 'you', so take the time to address 'you' and get help if your are bleeding.

I can remember many years ago, boarding an aeroplane for a mission to India. I was tired, worn out physically and emotionally but yet I was going to serve the people in India. I knew they expected so much from me. I had been to India in March the same year and after the many miracles and breakthroughs in people's lives, felt compelled to return in November of the same year. "The show must go on" or should it? The trip went really well and many lives were impacted. It was only years later that I realised I was bleeding and that I was a victim of the 'talent trap'. I knew I was gifted but I lacked wisdom.

Business as Usual

How many times have you seen major refurbishment taking place within a shop but a sign is still placed outside stating, "business as usual"? How safe would it be for you to enter the shop? This is often how our lives can be. Major repairs are needed but we continue to allow others to take from us. **Profit is not genuine when it involves neglect.** The shop that ignores the safety of its customers for the sake of profit has neglected the safety of its customers. There is nothing wrong is having a period in your life where you emphasise time for release, replenishment and repair. Release enables us to take time out of a pressure situation. Replenishment enables us to replace what has been taken out of us and repair enables us to receive healing for those things that have been broken within us.

In order to survive, people in the talent trap take 'pain killers'. There are so many things that can temporarily take away the pain but never remove the source of the pain. If you take pain killers for migraine, your pain might be removed but there are no guarantees that you will never have a migraine headache again. Many talented people in today's world are in pain and need loving help. Pain in medical terms often falls into two categories.

Acute Pain: Short-term pain that is easily identifiable and normally responds well to medication.

Chronic Pain: Pain that has lasted six months or longer and is often constant or intermittent. Chronic pains are normally more difficult to treat and amazingly do NOT help to prevent the body from receiving injury.

When talented people are trapped, their pain often becomes chronic!

The Bible tells us of a unique judge called Samson. A man of incredible strength who could fight an entire army. Samson from the moment he was born was destined to be different and dare I say famous. However, his internal struggles with his emotions were not addressed by himself, his parents or friends. In my view he was a man in pain. Most of his battles were personal battles and they did not serve to help anyone other than himself. Eventually, Samson's personal struggles were exploited by the Philistines. In retrospect Samson needed guidance, mentoring, counselling but the major issues in his life were camouflaged by his great strength. It was his enemies (the Philistines) who saw he had a weakness in the area of women and therefore used a woman to reveal the secret of his great strength. Samson had a great talent but very little discernment. Samson could have done with a real friend.

Talented people need true friends around them and beside them, people who will tell them the truth. The truth may hurt but it is a wound that will help them to become whole! You may have friends around you but being around you doesn't always give people insight into your life unless they are beside you. Many talented people build an entourage of people around them and have no one beside them. A true friend must be permitted to speak to you and often help you to come out of the talent trap and receive the love and help you need to be whole.

Talent can hide major problems for a while but more dangerously talent can cause a problem to be camouflaged. When something is hidden, it is generally not seen and must be searched for. However, when something is camouflaged, it is possible for something to be literally in front of our eyes but because it is camouflaged, it cannot be identified. In other words, it is hidden from our eyes through innocence and ignorance.

Key

1. Remember the 'talent trap' is designed to bring you to a place of destruction, so don't delay, break free today and let your talent wait on you. Try to implement the principle of release, replenishment and repair.
2. Be honest about the things that have been hidden behind your Talent.
3. Ask someone you can trust to tell you what they see about your life; they might just reveal something that had been camouflaged!

Proverbs 27:6 "Faithful are the wounds of a friend but the kisses of an enemy are deceitful".

Is Your Blood Speaking?

When a person is 'bleeding' from the soul, where ever they go and whatever they do, they will leave blood stains. I use this term to describe the tiny minute piece of evidence that reveals the truth of what is going on inside a person. You can still be brilliant at your job, fantastic at home and faithful in Church but in everything you do you are losing a drop of blood. In some cases you have left a blood trail. In counselling a lady, I realised that there were some childhood issues that needed to be addressed. I asked her to outline major incidents (good and bad) from the age of five to twenty one years of age. The place where internal bleeding is taking place is important because it is possible to bleed in the brain, lungs or stomach. It was heartbreaking to see that she had a 'blood trail' right throughout her life. Her father had neglected her and her peers rejected her. After each incident a part of this young girls' life was deposited and now as an adult she found it difficult to trust men and build sound relationships. Even though she was now a grown woman, the little girl of five years old was still crying out!

'Blood stains' are parts of your soul that secretly cries out in pain, usually after you have given to or served others. I can recall many years ago preaching at a crusade in India. Many people made a commitment to Christ, were healed and delivered. A few years previously, I knew that something within me was hurting but I thought that I just couldn't take the time out to investigate further. However, after this particular meeting, I felt really low and vulnerable to negative thoughts. It was as if after ministering, my soul was there for all to see, I was afraid. I remember going for a walk late that night hoping that this would shake the feeling off but it intensified. I prayed and prayed but it was as if God didn't respond. What was going on? The reality was that I had poured out so much to others in ministry that I was now close to breaking point. The years of overcoming some of the challenges of pastoring people, being let down and experiencing many disappointments had been camouflaged by my determination to persevere. God began to show me all the meetings and counselling sessions I had conducted over the years for others. He reminded me of the transformed lives but He also showed me how each time I had served, I had bled. I lost a little more blood. My friend, being busy and giving more to others will not stop your bleeding. My passion to give was partly my way of coping. I am not sure how long I could have continued to bleed without something serious happening but it was clear that I was now accountable to the revelation I had received about myself. **Self revelation makes you accountable to do something whereas ignorance affords you a degree of innocence but not an exemption from pain!**

We need to see the warning signs. It saddens me to read or hear of people with great potential falling from integrity as I always ask the question "why didn't anyone see them bleeding"? Most human beings can lose between 10-15% of their total blood volume without fatal consequences. The question is," how much have you lost over the years"? We need to act now. Listen to the way you speak about life, people and things. The Bible tells us that "Out of the abundance of the heart, the mouth speaks" .If you listen carefully, you will realise someone who is bleeding is indirectly asking for help or trying to get your attention. Every time you bleed emotionally it is unique because no one is exactly the same as you. When you bleed naturally, it is unique because your blood carries your own genetic and chemical make-up and history, which we call D.N.A.

I remember a mature Christian lady who from time to time would ring me up and share with me about the need for more fellowship in the church and the need for me as her Pastor to be more like a father to her. The lady was very faithful and even offered to organise several activities for increased fellowship. However, after one particular conversation, I asked her about her about her natural father, she burst into tears and expressed the years of loneliness and pain. She had been bleeding but the evidence was not in her actions but her words. What appeared to be a request of fellowship for others was actually a way of creating a service of healing for herself. Be conscious of the things you complain about in others because they can actually be the things you need for yourself.

The following question may sound strange but do you secretly desire to be someone else? Do you role play based on someone you have seen in your work place, family, Church or TV? What characters in films, plays or stories do you feel drawn to? I used to think that these kind observations were just trivial until I saw how the life of a dear friend evolved.

Mark was a great friend, one who had a great heart. I noticed that he modelled himself on a particular film character who was always fighting against extreme obstacles. The film character lacked academic qualities but was a great sportsman who showed tremendous heart. Amazingly Mark worked hard in the gym to develop a physique like him, talked liked him and even looked like him! He had submersed himself into this melancholy character adored my millions on the big screen. Mark was simply living out a life that he could identify with, he was crying out for help but no one seem to hear him.

When your blood is speaking you find it difficult to express what you are feeling and you might even find that you end up apologising for what you just said after several conversations. Your heart will usually speak quicker than your head! In other words before you have time to really think about what you shouldn't say, you've said it. Anger is a common element of bleeding because it feeds off three common things; injustice, rejection and frustration.

When we understand these facts we will hopefully begin to identify people around us each day who are bleeding. When I travel on a plane and find the stewardess grumpy and rude to me, it could be her way of venting her anger about her pay or working hours (frustration). When the shop attendant can't be bothered to help you find an item, it could be their way of venting their anger in response to their low pay (injustice). When a teenager rebels against authority it could be their way of responding to rejection.

In life when people are bleeding they suffer the one thing that pushes them even further away from getting help and this is 'rejection'. When the waiter in the Restaurant, or worker at a food check-out desk is reported to the manager for having a bad attitude towards the customers, they will normally lose their job or be avoided my customers. As a Christian Leader, I target rejected people and try to help them because I can hear their blood speaking through their attitude and behaviour. When you are leading a congregation it is easy to discourage contentious members of your congregation to relocate. I remember someone telling me about a woman that was attending my Church and how divisive she was at her last Church. It would have been easy to reject her but it didn't take me long to realise that through her rebellious nature and anger, her blood was speaking. Her rejection of authority was not personal to me or the Church but stemmed back from the misuse of authority she had suffered in her life many years ago.

I remember hearing several messages from an anointed preacher over a period of time. Many people were empowered by his sermons. However, there was a common theme of rejection to all his sermons and in my view there were 'blood stains'. Unfortunately he never addressed the fact that he was bleeding and eventually left his wife and ministry. Many people who knew his wife, knew that for all the years they were married, nothing his wife did was accepted by him. If you're leaving blood stains it is not too late to stop bleeding.

I remember once trying to change a water valve in my house. In order to do this successfully, I needed to drain the water system. I turned off all the water mains valves I knew about but for several hours the water system continued to be filled with water. Things only changed when I found a hidden isolating valve that would override all the other water valves. Once I knew where to close down the valve, the flow of water stopped and the water pressure decreased. It was my experience as a former engineer that enabled me to find the solution and stop the water. When you are bleeding, you need to find the course of action that will bring closure to your issue.

Begin to do an audit trail over the last few years of your life and if you can identify times you have bled ask yourself, "did I get healed"? The following is an example of what I call life stops. We can all bleed at different 'stops' in life. Some things may upset you but not everything causes you to bleed. Imagine travelling on a bus or train. When you decide on a destination, you often have to stop at places you do not intend to visit but need to pass through.

Stop 1: Discovery and Exploration. Every one has stops in their life where they discover things about themselves, about life and the people around them. People then tend to explore and investigate the things they have discovered. This can take place in our formative years or even in late adulthood. What we discover and explore can be negative or positive. When a person discovers that that they are not loved or appreciated, they can then often be led to explore ways to leave that relationship or environment. When a child discovers that they are being abused by those around them, they will often explore ways to escape. When a young man or woman discovers principles of success they will invariably explore ways to become successful. Conversely, when a child discovers the life of crime embarked on by his or her parents brings in wealth, they can seek to explore and experience that life for themselves. Therefore not everything we discover must be explored but simply clarified.

Stop 2: Acceptance and rejection. Everyone has stops in their lives where they will make decisions regarding what they accept and reject. If this is indeed everyone's prerogative, then we must also accept that others will make decisions regarding accepting or rejecting us. We often see rejection only as a curse but this is generally inaccurate. Acceptance can also be a curse!

If we behave in an inappropriate manner and are destructive in our interaction with friends, is it a good thing to have people to never challenge our behaviour and accept us the way we are?

Ideally, would you want to continue working for a company that covertly disliked you and were only continuing employment of you, until they found someone else? Would you stay in a relationship where some one was happy to receive your financial commitment to a home but inwardly rejected you from their heart?

Stop 3. Joy and tragedy. Is there anyone on the face of the earth who is exempt from this stop? However, I would suggest that there are some people who demonstrate no visible reaction to things that have brought them pain or joy. It is possible to cry tears of joy and tears of grief. Outwardly the signs are the same but inwardly there is a distinct difference. One of the things that does irritate me are drivers who blow their horn at me when the traffic lights are still red! When you are at this 'stop' take some time to process your emotions and don't allow those that are impatient around you to move you on before you have.

If you have faithfully applied yourself to the previous chapters of this book, then there is a strong possibility that you are ready to move towards a prognosis, that will help you to consider the things you need to do now to embrace your long-term healing and recovery.

Key

Never ignore the words your body 'speaks'.
Take time to interpret your pain. Pain is a language.
Don't be afraid to retract things you have said, when you realise you only said them because you were bleeding.

Psalm 139:14 "I am fearfully and wonderfully made...."

It Did Matter!

This is perhaps the most important chapter in this book, simply because there will be something that matters to everyone regardless of how small or big it may be. The classification of what does and does not matter to us is a matter of personal choice. There is a difference between effect and affect.

The things that effect us, are generally described as the things that bring about physical, material or external changes and these changes, change outcomes. An example of this is when someone loses their job; their employment status changes and personal circumstances invariably change. Another example are the effects of a new Superstore in a town that cuases the smaller Convenience stores to lose business and eventually close.

The things that affect us are generally described as the things that change us internally, emotionally. When someone we love dies, their death will effect our everyday life but emotionally and even mentally we will be affected. There must be a genuine review of your heart, a genuine analysis of what has affected you and when you decide that what transpired did matter, you will be able to address the emotions attached to the event.

John was an ambitious office worker within an engineering company. He had been on the company for many years, practically from School and had been promoted to work in the busy and vibrant sales office. Eventually John was promoted to the position of Sales manager over a team of twenty sales engineers. Away from work, John was a dedicated husband who absolutely adored his children. However, during an economic recession, John was called to a meeting with his sales director who informed him that there needed to be several redundancies throughout the company. The sales department was one of the key areas where the work-force needed to be reduced by 50%. John was given the task of assessing who were the best ten Sales engineers and then making the rest redundant. John was asked several times by his Sales Director if he was happy to do this because if he wasn't, he would find someone else. The Sales Director was conscious of the fact the John had a very close relationship with all the engineers and some were his personal friends. John was adamant that his personal relationship with the Sales engineers wasn't an issue. Over the next month John interviewed all the Sales engineers in order to be clear about who should really stay on the company. John then eventually sat down individually with the ten Sales engineers who would be made redundant and broke the news to them. There was a wild mixture of emotions from the sales engineers ranging from anger to fear. Many of the engineers felt a sense of betrayal due to the close relationship they had with John. During one of these meetings, one of the engineers verbally abused John. John however, remained calm and collected. Several weeks later the Sales Director asked John how he was, especially after the verbal incident with one of the sales engineers. John replied "I'm fine, it really doesn't matter what he said".

One year later John was signed off from work with chronic depression. Unknowing to his work colleagues, John had starting drinking excessively in order to cope with the stress of making many of his personal friends redundant. He had become agitated with his children and aggressive towards his wife. The truth behind what happened to John is the fact that making his friends redundant and receiving abuse from one of the engineers, actually mattered to him and the whole process affected him. In John's own words,

"In the week I had to make those ten engineers redundant, I experienced emotional pain in each meeting. Each meeting became more intense and now I live with the pain every day. I just didn't want my Sales Director to think I wasn't strong enough for my job".

We all need to move to a place of complete honesty and accept that things really matter to us and some of the disappointments and challenges in life have caused us to bleed. I know in times past, I had become confused with the positive effects of an incident that still left me seriously affected. I remember breaking a relationship with a friend who had shared many great experiences with me. I wouldn't say he was a very close friend but he was a friend. I had noticed over a period of time that he had become very critical of others, had began to compromise his integrity in various ways and was slowly undermining my trust. When the friendship finally ended, I felt the positive effects of him not being in my life but was surprised how I was affected by the whole process. **I then needed to take the time to process my emotions and put effective closure on the situation.**

There is one thing that will never be taken away from us all until we leave this earth and it is something called, 'challenges'. Life is full of challenges and challenges essentially test our resources and capacity as a person. However, I am amazed at how many people lie about the effect losing a challenge had on them! Whether it is playing an electronic game or a game of cards, for some people, it always matters if they win or lose. On the surface, this kind of attitude appears to be the hallmarks of a potential champion or world-beater. However, this kind of mind-set can make life too intense and sometimes too serious! I realised that after being married for a few years, the things I was initially adamant were crucial for me to be happy in the marriage, as time went on, faded away into insignificance. Are you someone that reacts as if the world is about to end every time there is a storm? I encourage people to choose their battles wisely by narrowing down what matters into three well known scientific categories.

Solids. These are the things are the foundations of who you are and are the things you have based your life and relationships on.
Liquids. These are the things that do matter to you but are flexible. In an ideal world it would be great for these things to met and achieved but you can live without them.
Gases. These are things that only for a set-time in your life, are important but are not worth getting too upset about because they will soon just disappear into insignificance. To give things in this category too much energy and time will generally lead to unnecessary pain.

Childhood is a time where we first decide what matters to us. You might be amazed what you can remember even back in your childhood and you might be even more amazed regarding the reason why you remember. People tend to remember events according to what mattered to them. Joy and pain are the two most common emotions that help us to remember people, incidents, times, events and conversations.

If you have found that you have been ignoring the things that really matter to you, it might be because someone dismissed your first response to something that did. **Negative words can often convince people into ignoring the things that should really matter in their lives.** People often speak negatively into the area of your life that they know will matter to you. They distort your thinking by crushing your first ever response or reaction to something that is important to you. Many times that first rebuff is enough to force people to internalise their feelings. Many people no longer share what matters because they believe that they were wrong to respond in that manner. At the age of eleven, I can remember my school teacher telling me my handwriting was like a gorilla in a cage! Maybe she thought that her comments would inspire me to write better but the truth is that her comments cause me to lack confidence in writing. I didn't try to confront her but I eventually confronted the emotion that was attached to the event and developed my own style of writing. I don't have the best handwriting in the world but I am no longer affected by what someone said. Maybe one day I will find my old teacher and let her know contrary to how I responded, what she said really did matter!

Key

Things matter to you for a reason. If you find that the reason is something that you need to address then once it is addressed what matters to you might well begin to change.

Psalm 61:2. "From the end of the earth I will cry to You, when my heart is overwhelmed; lead me to the rock that is higher than I".

Don't Cut Yourself!

When you buy a set of plasters to keep in the medical cupboard at home, don't be surprised if the majority of times you need plasters are for the times you injure yourself!

This chapter may be a bit difficult for you to read but you need to consider what you are doing to your self that is causing your soul to bleed. If you do not stop 'cutting' yourself, your chances of recovery will be reduced if not eliminated. As a society, it is easier for us to think of there being a perpetrator and victim when injury has taken place. However, it is possible for the perpetrator and victim to be the same person. I would like you to consider the following points that might appear extreme but are common.

1.**Protection**. Gardening without gloves? Seems trivial but how many times have you been cut by a sharp branch or prickly thorn, simply because you wore no protection gloves. Do you run into situations without protection? As an apprentice engineer, I use to wonder why I needed to have so much protection when working on certain items of equipment like Cooling Towers and Boiler rooms. There were times when my engineer and I, were under great pressure to finish certain jobs on time. However, I am glad that we didn't compromise in regards to protection, as years later many people have become seriously ill, even fatally ill, due to their exposure to the bacteria from old cooling towers and the harmful dust of asbestos in old boiler rooms. To continually leave yourself exposed to potential injury is 'cutting' yourself!

2.**Naïvety**: I hope you are still reading! You can cut yourself by being naïve! It is possible for someone to be bright but still naïve. Naivety in many respects deals with a lack of critical judgement, discernment or wisdom. When we are naïve, we can believe every promise, not recognise when something is dangerous or dead and make major decisions on limited information. When we are naïve we can be sincere but sincerely wrong. When we are naïve we can confuse a new experience with progress or change with something that is just presented in a different package! Sometimes we are constantly having bad experiences that we convince ourselves are helping us to progress in life, when in reality are on a merry-go-round.

3.**Relationships**. Proverbs 6:32 states, "He who commits adultery with a woman lacks understanding and does harm to his own soul". There are people we will inherit into our lives. They are there by divine choice (father, mother) however; you can generally choose your friends and those you desire to be in close relationship with. Bad prolonged relationships will eventually cause damage to your soul and sometimes you have to accept that your choices have brought more distress than joy to your life. It may be hard for you to accept, but some of the relationships you have formed throughout your life have not been healthy or genuine. Ink cartridges for mainstream Printers can be very expensive. However, rival suppliers have made replacement cartridges that are compatible with many mainstream replacements. Having tried to save some money, I purchased one of these compatible replacement cartridges only to be warned by my computer that 'I was not using a genuine manufactures cartridge and that future use could damage the printer and reduce the quality of prints". The text box that came on the screen read, "please click yes to continue or no, to stop printing". Do you get the point?

4.**Communication**: How many times do we 'cut' ourselves by sharing valuable information with the wrong people? Words are very powerful and every time you share a word from your heart, you are releasing a part of your heart. Samson told his secret to Delilah and was subsequently defeated and afflicted. It is great to be open but many times people can talk too much and share too much to the wrong person. The wrong person will generally cause your own words to afflict your own soul. The tragedy is that your mouth was the perpetrator and your soul became the victim! Jesus used a model for communicating three thousand years ago that many major organisations use today. There were things Jesus spoke openly to the crowd, to His disciples and then to a selected three from His twelve disciples. There are at least three levels at which information is transmitted, shared and stored.

Corporate: This is the level you can safely say anything to anyone about. If they want to spread what you have shared, just point them to the page of the book you have already written covering the very subject! This level is simply what everyone sees or knows about you.

Team: This is the level of friendship; those that make-up your life and often contribute to its well-being. They are people that add to you. This level is simply the level what you are happy to tell people about your life rather than let them just hear about your life.

Personal: This is the level at which you share without fear or shame. You will normally know the people that are called to this level because they tend to reciprocate openness and trust and the same level as you.

5. **Comfort and Cure**: Every body needs comfort in the time of challenge, concern and grief. However, you can inadvertently cut ourselves by pursuing comfort at the expense of a cure. When a person is worried or stressed they may find some 'comfort' in drinking a whole bottle of wine or finishing a pack of cigarettes. However, when the bottle and the pack of cigarettes are finished, neither one has solved or cured the problem that caused the concern. How many people have embarked on a night of passion because they were depressed and when the event was over, realised the depression remained? If this is you, you are causing yourself to bleed. The time has now arrived for you to seek healing not just comfort.

Key

Believe that you can recover.
Find someone who allows you to share. Remember the person you share with, might not be the person to help you complete your recovery but they might be the person to help you start the journey.
Don't allow your current actions to exasperate or perpetuate your pain.

Proverbs 16:24 "Pleasant words are like honeycomb, sweetness to the soul and health to the bones."

Getting Past Your 'Never Agains'

In medical terms 'traumatic bleeding' is caused by some type of injury. The injury may be from what is termed a blunt trauma assault as with a club, fall, motor vehicle accident or penetrating trauma as with a knife or gun. The Greek word for 'wounds' in the New Testament Bible is actually the word *trauma*.

Has anything happened to you that has caused you to confess that you will never trust or love anyone again? Maybe you are experiencing traumatic bleeding. If you have been unfortunate to be involved in a car crash there is a decision that every driver has to make after the crash. Will I drive again? Surviving the crash is only half the challenge. What you feel you can no longer do after the accident is even more crucial. How many people have vowed never to go to church again, never to love anyone again, never to help anyone again, never to be in ministry again, never to work for anyone again because they have a wound (trauma) from which they are still bleeding? **In order to have a good chance of recovering,**

you will have to change some of your 'never agains'. Your prognosis will not be positive if you block up pathways for healing with inner vows.

During a mission trip to Kenya, I made friends with a Christian business man who had survived the 1998 Nairobi terrorist bombing where many people sadly lost their lives. He shared very graphically the moment the bomb was detonated as he worked on the top floor of an office building. He suffered severe injuries and saw many fatalities. He said that his biggest battle was not trying to walk down several flights of stairs (the lifts were disabled) with blood streaming down his eyes but the courage he needed years later to work in a high rise building again. What he needed to overcome, was the trauma of the incident not just the incident itself. Today he still has a few scars and some permanent damage to the muscles in his hands but he has been able to change his 'never again'. Even the most safety conscious person will bear a mark, great or small on their body that reminds them of an accident they were involved in. We all have marks but the wound must be healed.

I can recall as teenager having an altercation with a boy at my first church. This was before I was a committed Christian. I was in Church but Church wasn't in me. This boy was younger than me and he had been provoking me for several weeks. I decided to do some 'ministering of my own', so after church I gave him a punch in his stomach (as mentioned before I wasn't a Christian). I thought that would be the end of him provoking me. I was devastated to find out that a few days later he was rushed to hospital with internal bleeding. I felt absolutely terrible, especially as I knew the family and his bigger brother and sister!!!

When I spoke to his mother and duly apologised I said something to her that still resonates in my heart "I had no idea that what I did would cause him to bleed". Many of the people that may have mistreated you or hurt you had no idea that they had caused you to bleed and we need to forgive them. Forgiveness doesn't always stop you from bleeding but is a giant step to experiencing healing

One of the ways to overcome trauma is to identify and focus on the emotion that impairs you not the person who inflicted the injury. One of the best examples of this is the actions of professionals when a football player gets injured through a foul during a match. The team mates of the injured player tend to vent their anger and focus on the offending player but the physiotherapist will identify the areas of pain, focus on the injury and apply the necessary treatment. It may have been a bad tackle that caused the injury but the focus must be to alleviate the pain. Injustice is a primary reason why people who have been hurt seek revenge on the perpetrator but revenge doesn't truly bring healing, if often just transfers anger.

GETTING PAST YOUR NEVER AGAINS'

There are times when saying "never again" is necessary but **far too often the words are used to form an inner vow that doesn't guard our heart but actually builds a wall around it.** You then find that people who really love you, have to fight to get close to you because they are coming against a strong wall. Remember if you say "never again", some things will never happen again, it means that history will never repeat itself in your life and some seasons of opportunity will never be accessed again.

Never is such a strong word, it is the 'full-stop' after a statement but saying never should not keep you from a better life, better relationship, healing, deliverance and joy. If saying "never", was to protect you then maybe it is safe to 'come out now'. If saying "never", was due to lack of trust, them maybe you can trust now!

Remember people can change and so do situations. When you are designed to be a particular way; perhaps you have a gift of hospitality, it is important to recognise that **your temptation will be to become the opposite of who you are by releasing an inner vow not help anyone again.** This action will often result in you causing more damage to yourself than to others. Don't suppress who you are, the more freedom you experience in being yourself the more comprehensive your healing will be.

One of the most important reasons for you to change some of your 'never agains', is in order to put closure on a traumatic episode in your life. As hard as it may be, you may just have to talk to 'that' person again in order to close the incident in your heart. This act doesn't always mean reconciliation or restoration but it can bring inner peace. 'Never agains', are sometimes necessary in order to prevent a repeat of certain unwanted events but it is important that they are protecting you and not robbing you of quality life opportunities. Are you missing out on a marriage, a business opportunity, a ministry or a friendship because of a never again? As a Christian I have learned to trust God in my decision making because I realise how easy it is to be impulsive when I am experiencing pain. **If you jump off a ship just because it is going through a storm then you might never know what you would have achieved or the places you would have gone to, had you stayed on board.** I remember taking a ferry trip to France with a few friends. The outward bound journey was great and the Channel was calm. However, on the return journey the ferry was violently hit with waves and wind. I had never experienced anything like it before. Glasses and plates in the canteen were being smashed and all passengers were told to remain seated. The normal forty-five minute crossing took about one and a half hours. One of my friends turned around to me and said "thanks for inviting me to France, but I will never travel by ferry again". The problem is that my friend would not only miss out on travelling to France again but any place that required her to travel by a ferry or cruise ship. This is one of the unique problems in saying 'never again', it normally excludes you from fresh opportunity.

The same old place!

The word 'again' can mean a return to a previous position, place or state. There are indeed times when it is not good for you to return to a previous position or place but sometimes overcoming an 'again' could give someone or something a second chance to do better! Do you have a fear of returning to the same old place? **When we return to a position, things can often be different because we have changed internally**. You need to ask yourself is it the place or the person within, that needs to change? I remember a young husband that had left his marital home on a few occasions due to various problems. At first he was adamant that he didn't want to return home again. However, after counselling him, he was able to return to the marital home because he had changed internally. The main issue was not the place but the person within. The very thing he said he would never do again, was changed because he let go of a vow he had made.

Key

Don't be afraid to try something again providing your attitude is different the next time round! Remember if you approach a situation with the same attitude you will get the same results.

Take the time to recognise, analyse, discuss and pray through all your ' never agains' and be willing to change the ones that would hinder your recovery after surgery. Maybe doing something one more time could be the difference between living with or without your pain!

Proverbs 23:18 "Surely there is a hereafter and your hope will not be cut off".

Jumping Out of the Wheel

Many of you may have seen an energetic mouse running inside an exercise wheel. However, this was the vision the Lord gave me regarding people who were in a cycle of pain and defeat. The Lord showed me that every so often someone would come along and motivate the person who was trapped in a cycle (running inside the wheel) to try even harder to come out of the cycle and as a result, they would put even more effort and energy into running (just like the mouse) . The reality of the situation, is that for as long as you are in the wheel you are still in the cycle and have made no progress, regardless of how fast you run. Cycles are normally made-up of problems and each problem aggravates and produces another problem that in turn eventually forms a loop, commonly known as a cycle.

Cycles don't end necessarily because you try but rather because you know how to end them. The best Christian sermons you will hear are not simply the ones that motivate you and have you shouting with joy but the ones that actually give you the "when and the how's". As a leader, I am always conscious of people not simply being excited by my sermons or mentoring sessions but leaving the meeting with the knowledge how to make progress and overcome obstacles. It can be frustrating attending an Anger Management course knowing that what you needed was an Anger Resolution course instead. Cycles also don't end because you enter into a time of positive confession telling yourself that the cycle does not exist. True positive or faith confessions do not lie about facts (what exists) but brings the fact or situation under the subjection of what we know to be true by way of our faith, or by what we know should be the ideal. If this is true, how do I end the cycle of bleeding in my life?

Take a chance and jump out the wheel! Jesus and the Apostles used this direct approach in their ministry by telling people to "rise, take up your bed and walk". Don't wait until the wheel stops turning. If you have ever been brave enough to parachute out of a plane you will know that the two hardest moments are the 'jump out' of the plane and the landing. Parachuting normally takes place at an altitude of 13,000 feet. You normally don't activate the parachute until you reach about 2,500 feet. **This means there is a period where you are 'free-falling'. A time when you let go of everything and you are no longer in control**. Even when your parachute is fully inflated you will be concerned about where you will land! When you jump out of a wheel or cycle there will always be an element of risk but it is worth taking it! In order to survive, you may have to jump out of a situation when it is at its most potent. I recently watched a film where a playwright was inadvertently detained on a ship in port. When he finally ended his meeting and ran out to the deck he realised that the ship had already left the port. Frustrated with his friend he said to him "I have just missed my rehearsal". His friend replied "if you loved your rehearsal enough then you would have jumped off and swam the short distance back to shore". How much do you love yourself? We sacrifice for others but do we sacrifice for ourselves? When Jesus said that we should "deny" ourselves He didn't say we should neglect ourselves (Matthew 16 :24).

Don't be afraid to stop what you are doing for a moment or even a season. In London if you travel on the underground trains or travel on major motorways, you will be used to trains and roads being closed and cancelled. During one trip on the motorway where the traffic was literally travelling at walking pace, I saw a sign that will help many people to 'jump out of the wheel'. The sign said "we apologise for any inconvenience but essential motorway maintenance is in progress". The question is, do you think that the government agency that employed the contractors to close a lane on a motorway considered the disruption to traffic, stress on drivers, extended journey times before they made the decision? Of course they did and even if they didn't, the need outweighed the inconvenience. I am a believer in individuals developing and building their character through life's challenges. However, when two boxers are in a ring fighting, the trainer will stop the fight if their boxer is taking too much punishment. Many times the boxer taking severe punishment, will not recognise the need to stop the fight and this is true for some of us. Jumping out of the wheel will give you time for essential healing regardless of the inconvenience. You will be amazed how quickly people start coping without you!

As a Pastor, I have counselled many people who have been involved in relationships. When the nature of the relationship becomes violent whether that be physical or emotional, I feel compelled to advice the individuals of the danger of staying in such a relationship. Many have felt trapped inside the wheel of a relationship. "How will I cope with being single again"?,

"Maybe I can cope with the violence for a little bit longer and then he or she will change", "what will people say, I can't leave the relationship"? Unfortunately some don't jump out of the wheel.

Are you stuck or trapped in a cycle? There can be a distinct difference between the two scenarios. When someone is usually trapped, they are being held in a place or position that they cannot find away out from. However, when someone is stuck, they can knowingly be held in a place or position by virtue of their own choices but yet cannot find the strength to overcome the things that has causes them to be stuck. In an instant, it is possible for a child to somehow push their head or hand through two parallel bars but then be stuck in a position where they are afraid to reverse the actions to get out of. It was easy for the child to push their head through the bars but much harder for the child to go through the conscious pain off pulling their head out! This is an important observation regarding people that need to jump out a wheel. It is usually easy to get into something but much harder to get out it. If you need to jump out of the wheel you will need to apply a greater force than the one that is holding you.

When a wheel is turning it produces a force known as centrifugal force. In Latin the word centrifugal is made up of two words *centrum* meaning centre and *fugere* meaning to flee. **It is time for you to flee from the negative things that have taken centre-stage in your life.** If you have ever been on a spinning Fair Ground ride you will notice that your whole body experiences a force that pushes you out from the centre of the revolving object. For some, the experience can be frightening or exciting. When we desire to flee from our wheel we are frightened because we have no idea where our decision to jump out of the wheel is going to take us, sometimes the changes can appear too quick! However, there are times when in order to preserve our lives we need to act quickly.

Jumping out of a cycle will require some things to stop. Why do many so many human beings have a problem with the word 'stop'? Maybe it is because the word is not an invitation but a command. One of the reasons why they have cameras in the U.K. at traffic lights is because of the increasing number of people who do not stop at traffic lights. Everyone is in a crazy rush and we often pay the price for our impatience.

There is a need for you to consider stopping some things but you need to plan ahead. Many years have passed since my successful driving test but I can remember one important aspect of the theory, 'stopping distance'. My driving instructor told me that when I wanted to stop I needed to start breaking early so that I did not lose control of the car through sudden breaking. However, he also taught me that in extreme driving situations, I needed to know how to make an emergency stop. In driving there are three main distances to consider and you can apply this to stopping some of the things that are a hindrance in your life.

Thinking distance: This is the distance and time at which you start thinking about stopping. Begin to think about how you can stop!

Breaking distance: This is the distance at which you start applying pressure to your breaks in the car. Start applying changes that will help you to change some key things in your life.

Stopping distance: This is the actual distance your vehicle stops at.

As mentioned, there are times when jumping out of the wheel requires an emergency stop but there are some dangers. When we desire to end cycles in our lives, I often advice people to do things gradually based on a principle I have seen in the ministry of Jesus called the 'displace and fill principle'. Whatever Jesus set people free from, was filled with a better alternative. When you suddenly end a long lasting relationship or suddenly give up smoking it is important to consider what will now fill the thing that you have displaced? This is why I believe that you are at your most vulnerable a month after you have made a major life decision. You begin to adjust and try to find better things to meet a need but during that time of filling, you can be tempted to change your decision. Maybe being in the 'wheel' weren't that bad after all"? Don't change a decision to stop something that you have effectively processed!

How many times do we wait for the perfect moment before we address what our own internal needs are? "I just need to organise the next conference", "I will just wait until the children are older", "I will just wait until the ministry is established", "I just need to finish this project". The perfect time is ALWAYS when you know you need to jump out of the wheel. Many times the cycle will break the moment you have learned to say no. This is because many great people who are bleeding are trapped within the deception of faithfulness. There are some people who continue to serve others regardless of what they are going through because they want to remain faithful but there are times when it is faithful to say "no". How many times have you had a work colleague come into work sneezing, coughing and spluttering every two minutes for the sake of being faithful to the company? The result being they have passed on their cold to others. They have only resulted in causing others to be off sick next week.

The reality is that millions of people are trapped in the 'wheel' and cannot find a way out. The following example may seem a little extreme but the point I am making is important. If you were travelling at 15 MPH in a vehicle that was out of control and heading to career of a cliff ,would you take your chances by staying in the vehicle and hope that the structure of the vehicle would protect you from a major impact? Or would you take a chance and jump out of the car while it was moving? This is the dilemma that many people are facing today. They know they are bleeding and if they don't get help there will soon be a mighty crash. However, the only way they can get help is to stop what they are doing within the 'wheel' and jump out. Jump out of the wheel, jobs will always be there, the career will always be there, be willing to face a few minor consequences. Staying in the car is potentially fatal whereas jumping out of the car might give you a few bruises and cuts.

The source

All cycles have a power source, in the same way a clock or watch may have a battery to keep it ticking. There are various things that can give power to a cycle but the most common power source is you! When you jump out the wheel the cycle has no more power over you. Power in physics in generally defined as being the amount of work or energy expended over measured time. The two things that cycles drain from you is energy and time but if you step out of the wheel you can begin to use your time and energy for positive things.

Take time out for you! Who told you the WHOLE world depended on you? Jump out the wheel today and let the rest of the world continue!

Key

It always take courage to jump out of a situation.
Recognise that some situations require you to jump not walk or crawl out of a situation.
Before you jump out of a situation consider what you are going to jump to!

2 Timothy 1:7 "God has not given you the spirit of fear but of love, power and a sound mind".

QUARANTINE

One of the best possible ways to prepare for your surgery is quarantine. Don't be surprised if you find yourself needing to take time to process thoughts and emotions without major distraction prior to surgery. This does not mean that your prognosis is bad, it just means you need to remember the need not to create additional problems through how you are currently feeling. Without a time of quarantine, you may hinder your long-term health because during this time you are at your most vulnerable. There are different types of isolation and quarantines. Certain types of quarantines are necessary in order to contain the spread of a disease. However, you can isolate a male Lion from a sick Lioness if you believe it is dangerous for them to mate. The Lion is still around other animals but not those that he could enter into fatal relationship with. Quiet- time before surgery is good and can normally be achieved by installing good boundaries and not walls. Boundaries are generally specific but walls keep out the good and the bad!

How many times have hurting people ruined a good relationship because they didn't go into quarantine? Quarantine comes from an Italian word that means, forty-day period. I think there is some wisdom in this definition as we need to take time in order to form new habits and ways of thinking. Going into quarantine is not just for your benefit but also for the benefit of others as you may have identified that within you there is something dangerous that if spread, could affect others. There must be a period of time where you do not expose yourself to potentially harmful situations prior to surgery.

When I was an engineer working for a large air conditioning manufacturer, there were times when I would need to put equipment in quarantine because we discovered a defect. The equipment stayed in quarantine until we had discovered the design fault, tested the equipment under customer conditions and signed the paperwork releasing it back into service. The equipment could not 'walk' into quarantine, so I enforced the quarantine. You must be the one that voluntarily goes into quarantine rather than having to be forced, so that the areas of your life that need to be healed and adjusted are completed without causing injury or damage to others. Equipment that had a defect could potentially put users at risk. Once again, I am not suggesting total isolation but the need to step back from the glare of everyone so that you can be prepared for surgery. I am also not suggesting that you could definitely infect others because your bleeding but you are more likely to do so amongst people that are not aware of your condition or do not know you very well. The following are five reasons why it is useful to have a time of quarantine prior to surgery.

To prevent offending others. You have reached a
   placed where you are ready for change and this is a
   great achievement. However, you are also at a place
   emotionally where your emotions are sensitive and
   heightened. I have realised that prior to my wife giving
   birth to our children, there were times when knowing

the true character of my wife was a great advantage in the delivery suite. I am not sure how a stranger would have perceived her! Perhaps they would have been offended. In my experience as a Pastoral counsellor, offence is one of the biggest hindrances to people getting healed. Having being hurt them selves, they often find it difficult to know they have unintentionally offended someone else because of what they are going through. Therefore, it is important out of your love for 'some' people around you, to step back from your usual level of interaction for a short period of time until you are able to effectively function around them.

To prevent spreading infection. There are times, when the people around us see us as their Mentor. Mentees seek the council and wisdom of their mentor but their principle way of learning is by observing the behaviour of their mentor and recording their words. Be aware that having a mentee around you during certain seasons of your life prior to surgery may not be wise as they may replicate your behaviour and attitude.

3. **In order not to complicate surgery.** There are times you can be unnecessarily distracted and these distractions can complicate surgery. In the medical field, complications are described as being the deterioration in a condition or the worsening of a problem due to various conditions. An example of this type of complication can be septicaemia, which can be the result of an infected wound. Complications can cause unwanted issues in your life and make the time of surgery prolonged.

4. **In order to be silent.** Don't miss your opportunity to be silent. In Law, the Right to silence, is designed to protect an individual under criminal investigation and interrogation,

from self incrimination. There are times when what you say during your time prior to surgery, could incriminate yourself as your pain can take your words out of context. The best friends you can have during this season, are the ones you can be silent around without continual explanation.

5. **To prevent others changing your mind**. Once you have made a decision to get help regarding your situation, don't reconsider your decision because of other people's opinions. Once you are in quarantine, you will have sufficient time to be absolutely sure that you want to follow-through your process of healing. People who are used to the old you as deep down as human beings we love consistency. When people generally see inconsistency, especially in the life of their friend, there is a tendency to encourage them to take the fastest route to recovery and steps toward what they consider normality. One of the biggest temptations is to go for a quick fix instead of going into quarantine where you can be thoroughly examined. I have worked in engineering for many years and I have observed the conflict between the need for sales and the need for product excellence. When you are only sales driven, it is not your main responsibility to ensure that the product is efficient and safe. However, those who work in the area of production, are responsible for producing a quality product. There can come a time when products are released too early from quarantine for the sake of not losing sales. You are not a product that must be marketed for the benefit of others but you are a beautiful work of art.

KEY

Going into quarantine can cause rejection but some forms of rejections are potentially good, as you only want those who are additions to your life to remain. You are about to take one of the most important steps in your life, it is better to be silent now and then to speak as a new person later.

James 1:19 "Let every man be swift to hear, slow to speak".

TIME FOR SURGERY

If you have been diligent in following the action points in this book, then you are ready for surgery. When the need arises for a skilled surgeon to open up a human body for exploration or surgery, there are some key principles to remember. The people around the patient must be wearing the appropriate clothing in order not to bring the germs and bacteria that everyday clothing has into the theatre. In addition to this, the instruments that the surgeon uses must be sterilised in order to prevent infection. You have now reached the point of decision; choices that will now change your life and begin to shape a new future. This is not a time to procrastinate. The word procrastinate is literally made-up of two words. *Pro* means for and *crastinus* means tomorrow. Everyone has things they would like to do tomorrow but remember tomorrow is ALWAYS a day away. It is now time for you to implement the things you have learnt through this book and this may involve letting go of things that you have become comfortable with or allowing something to die that was draining you.

This surgery is about you and you are going through this surgery for the benefit of you. When you start to focus on yourself, it can be a strange experience. This doesn't mean you make yourself an idol but your life will drastically change when you recognise your God given value. Many people only see themselves in a mirror a few times a day but never look long enough to address the person behind the face. When God started speaking to me about me, it was really uncomfortable partly because I had become an expert at bringing others to a place of change and breakthrough and not myself. When you are preparing for surgery you might ask yourself many questions. "How will I be when it is over"?, "Is it life threatening"? " Do I really need to have it"? I have realised as a Christian and a former engineer, that things very rarely fix themselves. We all would love instantaneous miracles and they do happen but many times we are destined to pass through 'surgery' so that dangerous things within our lives can be corrected and if necessary, removed. Through surgery we can develop a new mind and a new perspective on life.

The people you interact with at this particular moment and the "words" that you receive are critical. If the wrong people are around, they can exasperate your issue and even if you have the right people around you, it is important they speak the right words to you. Remember not every person on this earth knows what they should and shouldn't to do when someone is having surgery. How many times has a man or woman visiting a friend who is awaiting surgery, persuaded the patient to have some unauthorised food because their friend seemed hungry? The result of which the surgeon has to postpone the surgery because the patient should only have been on liquids! We need people around us who will give us what we need not what we want. Being on liquids prior to surgery can be hard but you don't need people who are going to feel sorry for you and end up postponing what has been appointed for you! **Don't take appointments for granted as you may have to wait a long time before another one is available.** In all our lives, we experience a *Kairos* moment. The *Kairos* in Greek, means, opportune or set time. If I miss the opportunity to do something at 2am tomorrow I will have to wait another 24 hours before I have a fresh opportunity to do something at 2am again! Don't miss your opportune time.

When surgery begins, we commit ourselves to the end of the process. Many times God brings people to a place where He can have our total attention. Nothing else at that moment of surgery is more important to you. Within every human being there is a pain threshold. Many people would never cry out for help to God or even a friend until they reach their personal threshold of pain. The pain gets our attention and the person who can help us gets our attention. Pain therefore in many respects is the 'hospital porter' that wheels you on a hospital bed to theatre where the surgeon is awaiting you. There are many people in your life that can help you at the point of surgery. Never allow anyone to open you up emotionally that do not have experience in the area of surgery you need. Would you allow someone to give you a kidney transplant that has never trained in that area? When my wife was expecting our first daughter, she had been in and out of hospital for three months due to bleeding. None of the doctors knew what the cause was. On the night my daughter was born, my wife had lost a serious amount of blood. The doctor on duty said that it was difficult to understand why this was happening as all the scans were inconclusive. However, as my wife became seriously weak, a new doctor came on duty and after one look at my wife, gave the order to rush her into theatre for an emergency caesarean. The doctor was an expert and her expertise possibly saved the life of my daughter and wife!

Are you ready? Let's go then!

Having done some basic research into surgery, I have realised that there are some basic steps that we can take in order to contribute towards its success.

Choose a good surgeon: It is imperative to use someone that is experienced in helping you in your particular area of need. Often times getting the best support will cost you but remember you cannot put a price on your well-being. Don't be one of those people who say " I would anything to be rid of this problem" and then when told it will cost so many pounds per our for a counsellor reply "Oh that's too expensive".

Educate yourself: Make sure you have taken time to analyse the various issues in your life yourself. Research the various types of help available and decide which one best fits your problem and lifestyle. This will often help the person who is helping you to begin dealing effectively with the key areas of your life.

Second opinion: Once you have decided on the type of support you need, get a second opinion from someone you can trust to be honest and totally objective.

Be positive: Believe that life will be better and the process of healing will be worth it once it begins. It can sometimes help to talk to others that have passed through a similar process and have become better people.

Commit to change: Life after surgery will never be the same, unless you allow it to. Commit to and take responsibility for, maintaining your health. Consider from time to time having counselling or attending some form of personal healing course or empowerment program that assists in developing you as a person. I have found that some people start counselling with me and fail to complete the designated sessions . Unfortunately they end- up worse because they disturbed the inner work that was taking place. Their heart had been opened up without any healing taking place. This leaves you in an emotionally vulnerable position.

I want to help stop the bleeding in certain areas of your life by encouraging you now to carry out seven acts of release. These are not exhaustive but are a great foundation for successful surgery.

Releasing people. Forgiveness releases those that have either deliberately or innocently caused you to bleed. It is time to stop people from hindering you. Unforgiveness can continue to tie you to people you truly want to let go of.
Releasing regret. Regret holds people to the memory of an unfortunate event. You cannot change the past only influence your future.
Releasing grief. Grief is a natural emotion that should be released and processed. However, when it is not released it affects your character and can affect your health.
Releasing anger. Acts of injustice happen to most of us but displaying no emotions at the time of the incident can be dangerous. Many times as an Adult the 'child' in us can still be angry with something that our parents did when we were a child. Many people absorb anger rather than releasing it in an appropriate and socially acceptable ways. You can be angry and not sin. Anger that has festered for years is no respecter of persons and can consume your rationale.
Releasing words. The biggest cause of internal bleeding is the constant replay of negative and destructive words people (or even yourself) have spoken into your life. There are many words that are spoken around us and over us but it is only the words that enter us that have

an affect. You need to release from your soul every word that has held you captive. Words you have spoken at the highest point
of your pain are some times the words that have cursed you and caused you to
bleed.

Releasing thoughts. Our thoughts eventually affect our ways. You may be holding onto thoughts of
revenge, rebellion even suicide but it is time to let those thoughts go. Thoughts have the ability to
consume us and it normally results in us getting sleep but very little rest. Thoughts can hold us in a place
of defeat or take us to a place of liberty. The renewing of the mind is only successful if that includes
your thoughts.

Release your fear: Fear is not just a perception of things, it is a stronghold. I would suggest that fear is
not necessarily destroyed but displaced and released. Fear exists but fear doesn't need to remain in us.
Fear can be created in us through a collection of thoughts but fear can also be received. When fear is
released from our being it is normally driven out by three keys things; power, love and good thinking.
You need to exercise strength. As a Christian, I draw strength and power from the Lord Jesus. For an
object to move there must be a superior force to overcome what is called inertia. In physics inertia is
defined as being the tendency of an object to resist movement when stationary. Fear will not go unless it
is moved by something stronger because fear has become comfortable within you! Remember that fear
needs a connective. Fear of, fear in and fear for. Identify the things you might have fear of, in and for
and release that fear by setting a deadline to do EXACTLY what fear didn't want you to do.

Key

Don't put any pressure on yourself to complete every area of release in one day. However, you will know within yourself when you have successfully carried out a release. There is no set-time for surgery to be complete as we are all unique before God. Surgery can be minor or major but the objectives are the same; wholeness. There will inevitably be changes but these changes can be managed. Change can essentially be:

Ignored. Ignoring changes in yourself and changes in your relationships sets a dangerous precedent.

Resisted. Changes that are inevitable should not be resisted as you ultimately drain yourself of vital personal energy and strength.

Received and managed. Changes to your personal life can with wisdom, be managed and harnessed for your greater good.

Jeremiah 30:17. "I will restore health to you and heal you of your wounds"

MY NEW WORLD

When you have experienced inner healing, it is a great feeling! You have become a new person in an old world! The new world I am talking about is the world through your eyes. One of the first signs of internal healing is the new and fresh perspective you will now have on the circumstances and events around you. **You can only truly influence the world you now see!**

Matthew 8: 22-26, tells the story of an incredible healing in the ministry of Jesus. A blind man is brought to Jesus in the hope that Jesus will heal him. Jesus uses unorthodox methods by laying his hands on him and putting spit and mud on his eyes. Jesus consequently asks the man, "what do you see", but the man responds by saying that he can only see men walking like trees. When you were bleeding within, there could have been so many things people spoke to you in love that you misunderstood and misinterpreted. From your perspective, men looked liked trees! However, the story doesn't end there and Jesus out of compassion touches the man again and the Bible says, "the man was restored and saw every man clearly". You need to know by revelation whether the relationships who had prior to being healed were simply because you were bleeding, whether the job you took was because you were bleeding or the ministry you started was because you were bleeding. If the answer is "yes", then there is a strong possibility that now you can see and discern things clearly, you might find that you really don't need certain people in your life at the level they currently operate.

Major revelations normally precede major decisions, so begin to anticipate 'change'.

Most people would not like to live in a hospital, yet they will stay in a hospital for as long as they require the expertise and supervision of doctors and nurses to make a full recovery. Over the years God has enabled me to help many hurting people who have visited my church. However, only a small portion of those people became members of my church. This was not because they were not grateful but because the only thing that tied them to my ministry was their condition not their vision. I have also seen cases where a non-Christian man has fallen in love with a Christian woman. During this time they appear to be building a strong friendship and the Christian woman is faithfully ministering to him in the belief that when he becomes a committed Christian he will become her husband. Unfortunately, in some cases when the man becomes a Christian and stops bleeding, he now 'sees' the Christian woman in a different light and finds that the desire he had towards her was a desire for someone to help him stop bleeding rather than for her to become his wife. Why is it that once a lame person can walk again they immediately throw away their crutches or stick? We must all be aware, that our role in some people's lives does not go beyond helping them to stop bleeding.

I would suggest to you that it is a good principle to be grateful for acts of kindness extended towards us and to make consistent efforts to keep good relationships. However, there are some people who have now served their purpose in your life or have served a role that now will evolve into something else.

Anti-natal midwives: Many midwives have become friends with the mother they helped during child-birth. The anti-natal midwife generally, does not continue her role with the mother beyond birth. Their main role is primarily to monitor, predict and manage the progress of the unborn baby and mother during labour. Midwives also offer education, advice and support. There are people who will help you during your surgery and their advice and support is invaluable.

Neonatal midwife: These midwives essentially ensure that mother and baby are progressing well and to also offer advice to parents regarding feeding, crying and any concerns the parents may have. They normally visit the mother and baby for twenty-eight days after the birth. It is important to have someone who will monitor your progress after you have come through surgery and made major life decisions.

There are **five keys** I want to give you regarding your new world that will enable you to enjoy your new world and guard against prolonged internal bleeding.

1) Entrances into your house. Proverbs 4:23. Most modern houses will have at least two possible entrances, normally at the front and the rear. Write down how many entry point's people have to your heart. Once you have done this honestly, analyse how safe your heart is having these people at these entry points and ask yourself the question "is their level of access to my heart safe?" You should now know who should have:

General access. These are people that you are confident have pure motives towards you. The words of these people are generally helpful and sensitive towards your needs.

Restricted access. These are people that can be slightly erratic in their behaviour and without warning can severely hurt you. You must regulate the amount of time and input these people have in your life.

No access. People you confidently know, do not have your best interests at heart and found their own self-worth through you bleeding all the time and you depending on them.

Gates

These are access points of your heart and life that people and things go through when they want to contact you. Most Gates are simply a 'means of access' or a 'means of exit'. Amazingly in computers a gateway is often defined as a piece of hardware or software that makes sense of various electronic signals and enables various computers to talk to each other. Your 'gate' is the place where you can decide upon who and what comes to the door of your heart. Many mornings the postman comes through the gates of many houses upon delivering letters. Just because the postman comes through the gate doesn't give them automatic access through the door of the house. Learn to know the people who are best kept on the pathway or garden of the gate.

Doors

Doors provide access into a house or a building. It is normally a movable structure that can bring someone from outside a building to the inside. Who do you need on the inside? Every person that is brought on the inside must have at least three things.

Value: We all need people who will be an addition not a subtraction in our lives.

Substance: We all need people of integrity and truth. People with character not just charisma.

Purpose: Why are they here? Purpose can often be seen by what they are inspired to bring into your life.

Anyone that breaks down your doors has violated security and ignored protocol. There are only two ways people can pass through your 'door' legally. One, if you open the door once you are on the inside and two if you give the door key for them to use. When you give someone the key to your front door it represents a high degree of trust as the person does not need to come and ask your permission to enter the house thereafter. I was once told by a security guard that one of best ways to reduce the security risk of a building was to 'limit' the amount of people who had the 'key' to the front door.

Walls

Walls are often boundary markers that provide a distinction of ownership. Without walls (boundaries) people don't often know what they own and where they can and cannot legally venture. Be careful not to build a 'wall' that serves as a blockage rather than a boundary. Most people simply need you to install clear boundaries but there are those for the sake of your well-being need strong clear boundaries that either restrict or withholds their access to you. Walls can cost you. The Great Wall of China remains one of the greatest man-made structures on the earth but it is estimated that over a million people have died guarding and preserving it.

It is important that you know the difference between guarding your heart and building a wall around it. Many people in trying to guard their heart block everyone out including the right people!

2) Love the model more than the role: Make sure you do not love fulfilling a role more than yourself! Many people who are bleeding inside have prolonged bleeding because they are trying so hard to maintain a role that they neglect the model (themselves). The reality is, if you breakdown emotionally, you are going to struggle to fulfil your role, therefore take more time to make sure the model (you) is well.

3) **Re-investment**. If you don't invest in yourself then how can you expect others to? If you have no time to spend money on yourself, develop your skills, be mentored, ministered unto, then your time management is wrong. No car can carry passengers indefinitely without the owner spending some money to get the car serviced. I often find the most vulnerable persons in a poor family are the mother and father, as they will often feed everyone else and go without food themselves. In certain parts of the world where I have carried out ministry ,I have seen where the only food that some young children receive is the breast milk of their mother. The loving mother will always give 99% of whatever food comes into the home to her children. However the mother is sometimes not aware that unless she eats healthily her breast milk will not contain the nutrients her children require. Invest in you!

4) **Maximum impact**. Now that you are healed, get ready to make maximum impact on the world but pace yourself. Now that you are not losing valuable strength and energy, you can now begin to channel all your energies in the right directions. Expect to hit your targets, to be more effective in your life. You may even find that your new strength surprises you and that you are not as tired or fatigued as before. I remember recently watching a World Championship Boxing match on television. The two boxers were well matched but after about three rounds into a twelve round fight, the champion noticeably changed his boxing style (conventional southpaw). The champion however, managed to win on points. In the post-fight interview the Champion said "from the 3rd round I broke one of my fingers in my right hand so that for the rest of the fight I changed my style so that my left hand could make maximum impact". When problems come upon you or something in your life is broken, simply make the adjustments and go on and win!

5) **Emergency numbers**. Every household needs to have a list of emergency numbers. It can be for a fire, gas leak, or criminal activity. Ensure that you have two or three people that you can be 'real' with when you sense you might be bleeding. There are people that don't need all the details, but the main facts. These are people that will not change their opinion of you, when you share your heart. These people don't necessarily need to be your friends but people of integrity, wisdom and love. Every person on this earth should have different levels of accountability and this helps to protect their personal integrity. In the U.K. most charities have Trustees. The general role of the Trustee is to provide impartial and objective oversight over the financial and administrative affairs of the charity. Oversight in our lives does not always mean control and in times of emergency we need people who will help us; not control us. Therefore be aware of who you call in

an emergency and ask yourself if they can remain objective. We all need emergency numbers!

Never doubt that you are healed, you are no longer bleeding. Just because you display emotions doesn't mean you are "back" to the emotional prison you were in. You're simply being human. You will always have emotions but through wisdom, your emotions will come under your authority. Before you can truly act differently you must begin to think differently and there are three key areas of transformation that must remain ongoing.

What you See.

When I was bleeding, I realised that there were times when I thought that certain people didn't love me when they really did! I believe one of the reasons for this was because of the way I saw the world, my perception ,the lens I was looking through. A broken lens will give a broken picture therefore ensure that your lenses remain clean. Practice having emotional dettox, where you can unwind and release tensions and any anxieties. Find a nice painting you can observe and after one minute write down what you saw in the painting. Then in 1 hour carry out the same exercise again. You will often see things the second time around that you didn't see the first time. Be willing to replay an incident in your heart before you respond to it. One of the main reasons for you noticing new things in the painting is because you have gained something very precious called experience. Perhaps the first time you are able to be yourself, share your heart and have someone affirm who you are, you will feel strange. However, the more you are yourself, the more you will begin to see things differently. Anyone that has a genuine appreciation for paintings has their eyes trained to know something of quality and can often see the message and statement of an artist in the painting that I innocently missed. Allow your sight to be transformed by good things and not bad things. Being sceptical in regards to certain issues can be useful but being cynical can be dangerous.

WHAT YOU UNDERSTAND.

Always seek to learn more about yourself, life and people. Life is indeed a daily classroom and experience is one of our teachers. As a Christian, I constantly pray to God and ask Him for more wisdom so that I can live my life with greater purpose and grace. As the world changes, so do people and you will need to understand how people think in today's world and people's current perception of life and love. Even if you are married, it is important that you grow with your partner and not get left behind in terms of who they have become. It is also imperative that you understand yourself. You have changed as a person and many times your brain is working overtime to rationalise your new actions. Don't be afraid to be systematic in setting times for self-analysis. Write down who you perceive yourself to be now, write down aspects of your behaviour and seek understanding regarding them. What you understand will effect what you hear physically and emotionally. One of the most important aspects of my ministry is understanding, especially when I am in a foreign country. I am blessed to have many fantastic interpreters that ensure my teaching and preaching is understood and correctly interpreted by the natives. My twin daughters are a great joy to me. Due to the fact they are still very young, I have noticed that they use one word they understand to cover the majority of their communication with me. If they are hungry, want a door to be open, desire a toy, the same baby word is used! Sharon and I, have to carefully interpret each request not by what we hear our daughters say but by what we interpret their words to mean on each occasion.

What you say.

What you say about yourself really matters. People are often the sum total of what they have spoken over their own lives. I am not talking solely about positive confession, I am talking about truthful conversations and confessions. Our success and healing in life is often lost or hindered in the casual conversations in life. Be disciplined in what you say to anyone about yourself and others. Your words can take you where your money cannot. Don't talk like a victim anymore, don't talk like your bleeding anymore, you're a new person a different character. I have noticed that there are certain actors who regardless of what characters they play in different films, they still sound the same when they speak. This can often confuse a regular movie fan like me as it can seem like you are watching the same actor and character in ten different films!

There must be transformation in what we say and we must continue to be transformed in our speaking so that our speaking reflects our maturity.

Change Position

Our position in life is crucial. This position is not purely social but is also emotional. There was a man I once knew who lived a few house away from my parents' house. Each day he sat by his window observing who was coming in and out of people's houses. If you ever spoke to him, his conversation would always centre on everyone's personal business! His conversation would not change until he changed his position.

Sitting in a chair at the window meant he could only see the community one way. Now you have been healed don't go back and sit in the same position. There will also be times when you will have to change "positions" in order to adapt to what is happening around you. I remember once watching a DVD at home with my two oldest children. My son complained that his sister was blocking his view of the television while she sat on my lap. If I asked my daughter to come off my lap, I knew there would be an issue and if I didn't address the issue our family evening would be spoilt. The simplest suggestion was for my son to move slightly along our large sofa and change position. Just by changing position an argument was avoided and everyone could enjoy the DVD! When you can change your position you can change apparent defeat into victory. Formula One racing drivers do it all the time, Boxers also do it all the time. In a split moment as they change their position, they change the whole outlook on the race and match. Remain adaptable and be willing to be transformed. There are three positions you should be aware of.

Offensive position: Always ready to attack.

Defensive position: Always ready to defend.

Neutral position: Always willing to judge each situation on its own merit and then to respond accordingly.

Try and adopt a neutral position!

Value your freedom. In nearly all aspects of life, freedom has cost someone something. For some it costs them their lives, others time and money. As a Christian, I try to never take for granted the price Jesus paid upon the cross for my freedom. His all embracing sacrifice has totally revolutionised my life.

I read some statistics recently regarding the prison population in the United Kingdom. I was staggered to find that in 2009 over 73,000 people are in prison every day of the week. They have lost the privilege to go where they want to go and interact with society, some serving life sentences have lost the privilege to fulfil their aspirations. I have been to minister to people within prison over the years and realise that there were those that were not impacted by the loss of freedom and had maintained the same mind-set that caused them to be sent to prison. However, there were those that were so desperate for freedom that you could be confident that they would employ the wisdom and lessons they have learnt through the experience of being behind bars. Your mind-set needs to change, a new paradigm for your thinking needs to be in place. It is so important that you value your freedom and previous mistakes are not repeated.

One of the ways you can motivate yourself to keep your healing is to remember the cost. This does not mean every week you wallow in self-pity but it means you can draw inspiration and strength from the determination and courage you have shown to reach a place of healing. Christians are encouraged to look forwards as well as backwards in their faith. This is because when we look backwards we remember the sacrifice of Jesus and when we look forward we draw strength in His promised return. Even if you are not a Christian this is a great principle. You must look back and forward in the hope you can avoid bleeding again.

We all owe someone a big 'thank you' for whatever freedom we have whether it is social, political or religious. All Indians owe Mahatma Ghandi for their independence today. This amazing man endured great oppression and even imprisonment in order to see India released from the British Empire. Many Afro-Caribbean's owe the Martin Luther King for his faith and determination in opposing public racial prejudice in America. Many of us who are able to fly across the world on mission, business or on vacation, owe Orville and Wilbur Wright for the time and money they invested in discovering the art of flying. This they finally achieved in 1903. Many Christians today would not have freedom of worship or maybe a Bible without the dedication of John Wycliffe and the boldness of Jan Huss who are both regarded as two of the most influential of religious reformers. John Wycliffe had a passion to translate the Bible into English so that the common people could read the Word of God other than the clergy. Jan Huss was excommunicated and burnt at the stake by the then Catholic Church for his liberating teachings. Many British citizens owe the men and women of the 1st and 2nd World war for today's freedom and democracy in our country. In the 1st world war it is estimated that more than nine million soldiers lost their lives on various battlefields for today's freedom.

Key

Value your freedom and live the rest of life being grateful that you are no longer bleeding. Someone has probably helped you on this journey to stop bleeding, now after reading this book, look for someone you can help too!

Proverbs 4:23 "Keep your heart with all diligence, for out of it flows the issues of life".

I'M FREE,

The chains have fallen off that were holding me,
Link by link was effectively broken,
As the real person in me was finally awoken.
Blinded by the worlds competitive edge,
I needed help but pretended I didn't instead.
I have unravelled the puzzle that never made sense,
I now see the relevance of my conscience,
My heart told me that 'bleeding' was not in my head but in my emotion,
I wanted to get back everything that pain had stolen.
Precious moments, opportunities I thought would never return,
Are now here in abundance for me to discern.
I have realised there is such a thing as 'happy ever after',
Just never thought that was written in my life's charter.
I can now look back on my life without regret,
Even though there have been many challenges , I now don't need to fret.
However ,I've learned to address issues when they arise,
If I need to take the time out to do so, I will no longer compromise.
I value my soul and who I shall become,

I can achieve many great things if I let God be number one.
Now I enjoy being who I really am,
The mask has been removed and I am beginning to understand,
Being transparent to some means being weak,
But for me finally, the truth I can now speak.
I have learnt how to change positions in order to again live,
I have found that the heart that I thought was dead is now responsive.
I can travel the road of life and make key decisions,
I am no longer influenced by people's doubts or derisions.
I can't explain why it took me so long to reach this place,
But I guess at my lowest point, it was time for me to find my ACE!
It is amazing what happens when you begin to truly share,
You begin to attract the genuine people around you, who really care.
They take the time to help you and to listen
And don't behave as if problems are for those of less distinction.
Internal bleeding could have eventually cut short my life,
With all the pain anger and inner strife.
But in truth the experience has served to make be wiser,
I now recognise that over every negative word, I am superior.
I have overcome challenges and removed certain threats,
I now know the difference between sacrifice and neglect.
I live not to survive but to live out God's plan,
I have so much to give to my fellowman.

If I do bleed again.. then it won't be for so long again, this is what I expect,
Because I now have the tools and the experience to detect,
I am stronger than I was before my surgery,
And I am ready to fulfil my goals because I now have the energy.

I have learnt that it is important to recognise my inner value,
so that those that don't can be diverted from my avenue,
Never knew the real value of crying out and interceding,
It is amazing how powerful prayer is when you need someone to help you stop bleeding!
I have found support and love in a perfect friend,
You may not believe but it is through His love, my heart can now extend;
Trust and friendship to a world that's hurting,
Just may be what I have learnt can stop some one else from bleeding!